Climbing
Mt. Shasta

second edition
Avalanche Gulch
"An Ascent"

SWS Mountain Guides

David E. Cressman
Timothy S. Keating
"JB" Brown

MOUNTAIN GUIDES

For information please contact: SWS Mountain Guides Publications, 210 East Lake St., Mt. Shasta, CA 96067. First Printing 1996. Second printing 1997. Third printing 2000. Fourth printing 2005. Second Edition 2011.

ISBN -13: 978-1468116854
ISBN-10: 1468116851

WARNING

**CLIMBING IS A SPORT WHERE YOU MAY BE SERIOUSLY
INJURED OR DIE.........
READ THIS BEFORE YOU USE THIS BOOK**

This book is a compilation of information gathered from numerous sources, and though the authors have taken reasonable steps to provide you with up-to-date information for your enjoyment of an activity for which you may not be skilled, neither the authors nor the publisher can assure the accuracy of any of the information provided in this book, including but not limited to; the topographic maps, other maps, route descriptions, and illustrations. Route descriptions in this book may be inaccurate or misleading due to the weather, snow conditions, and the changes throughout the seasons. If you have a doubt as to where a route leads, you should not commence unless you are sure you can go safely. In this book the route ratings are referred to as "technical and non-technical." Also, ratings of climbing difficulty and danger are always subjective and depend on the physical characteristics; experience, technical ability, confidence, and physical fitness of the climber who supplied the rating, do not be lulled into a false sense of security by the difficulty rating. The significant elements of risk associated with hiking, mountaineering, rock climbing, alpine skiing, ice climbing, and walking on glaciated terrain or surfaces (collectively referred to herein as "activity") cannot be eliminated without destroying the unique character of the activity. The same elements that contribute to the unique character of the activity can be cause for injury and the loss of life. Therefore, be **warned** that you must exercise your own judgment on where a climbing route goes, its difficulty, and your ability to safely protect yourself from the risks of climbing.

Examples of some of the risks are:
1. Heat related illnesses including heat exhaustion, heat stroke; and cold weather related injuries including hypothermia, frostnip and frostbite which may result in loss of limbs, digits, and/or permanent scarring.
2. Risks associated with climbing up or down or traversing on rock, snow, or ice.
3. Altitude related sicknesses including acute mountain sickness, pulmonary edema, cerebral edema, and/or retinal hemorrhage.
4. An "act of nature" which may include avalanche, rock fall, crevasse fall, inclement weather, high winds, and severe heat and cold.
5. Faulty use of equipment, or not using the equipment, or not knowing how to use the equipment.

By reading, using, or applying any part of this book, you agree to assume responsibility for the risks identified herein and those risks not specifically identified. You acknowledge your use of this book and your participation in the activity is purely voluntary. You acknowledge that no one is forcing you to participate in the activity, and you elect to participate in spite of the risks. You assume full responsibility for yourself, including any minor children for which you are responsible, for bodily injury, accidents, illness, death, loss of personal property, and expenses thereof as a result of the inherent risks and dangers which may occur as a result of your negligence and/or your participation in this activity. You hereby acknowledge that you have read, understood, and accepted the responsibility involved with the incumbent risks, and further acknowledge and agree that no responsibility of any kind will be placed on either the authors or the publisher by yourself, your heirs, assigns, personal representative, and estate, for yourself and all members of your family including any minors accompanying you, for any occurrences related to your participation in the activity. You should not depend on any information contained in this book for your personal safety. Your safety depends on your own good judgment, based on experience and a realistic assessment of your climbing ability as well as weather and route conditions. If you have any doubt as to your ability to safely climb a route described in this book, do not attempt it. The following are some ways to make your use of this book safer.

CONSULTATION: You should consult with someone that has climbed Mt. Shasta as well as U.S. Forest Service personnel, Wilderness Rangers, National Weather Service websites, Avalanche information hotlines, and mountain guides about the current difficulty, skills needed, and danger of a particular climb prior to attempting it.

INSTRUCTION: The authors strongly suggest that you take a Basic Mountaineering course from a qualified mountaineering school or instructor such as SWS Mountain Guides. You should engage an instructor or guide to learn safety techniques and to become familiar with the routes and hazards of the area described in this book.

PREPARATION: You must be physically and mentally able to participate in the activity and use the necessary equipment. You must be safety conscious and acknowledge that wearing a UIAA approved helmet may be a basic safety precaution with respect to preventing head injury. You must acknowledge that if during the activity you experience fatigue, chill and/or dizziness, your reaction time may be diminished and the risk of accidents increased.

REVIEW SAFETY: You must read and then review the Mountain Safety chapter in this book and obtain current information on those topics. You must thoroughly understand the risks and hazards discussed about the sport of mountaineering and those that pertain to the Avalanche Gulch Route as well as other routes when climbing on Mt. Shasta.

THERE ARE NO WARRANTIES, WHETHER EXPRESS OR IMPLIED, THAT THIS BOOK IS ACCURATE OR THAT THE INFORMATION CONTAINED IN IT IS RELIABLE. THERE ARE NO WARRANTIES OF FITNESS FOR A PARTICULAR PURPOSE OR THAT THIS BOOK IS MERCHANTABLE. YOUR USE OF THIS BOOK INDICATES YOUR ASSUMPTION OF THE RISK THAT IT MAY CONTAIN ERRORS AND IS AN ACKNOWLEDGEMENT OF YOUR OWN SOLE RESPONSIBILITY FOR YOUR CLIMBING SAFETY.

DEDICATION

"We dedicate this book to the memory of all persons who have been injured or lost their lives on Mt. Shasta. Hopefully, the information presented here will make future climbers safer and aware of the hazards of mountaineering."

SWS MOUNTAIN GUIDES

ACKNOWLEDGMENTS

Steve Lewis, Author of the first editions of "Climbing Mt. Shasta": Thanks for all your hard work and giving SWS Mountain Guides the opportunity to author the second edition.

Dan Towner, Wilderness Ranger, Mount Shasta Ranger Station: Dan supplied us with the statistics regarding the Wilderness permits. We want to give him special thanks for his work as a Wilderness Ranger on Mt. Shasta.

Siskiyou County Sheriffs Search and Rescue: The volunteer members of the Search and Rescue crew should be given the highest award in the county for their past and continuing efforts in rescuing lost or injured climbers on the mountain.

Dennis Freeman, Director of Library and originator of the Mount Shasta Collection: Dennis has been a great asset for allowing research in the Mount Shasta Collection at the College of the Siskiyous Library in Weed, California.

Stacy Smith, Special Use Officer, Mount Shasta Ranger Station: Stacy Smith took quite a bit of time over the years updating us with the ever changing rules and regulations that are taking place within the Mt. Shasta Wilderness area. Thanks for keeping us all up to date!

Nick Meyer and the Mt. Shasta Climbing Ranger Staff, who risk their lives daily to make sure that both the guides and public, can climb safely.

Emily White-Keating, Emily Sagalyn, and Alana Cressman, for all the time we have been gone pursuing our dreams guiding in the mountains. It takes a special woman to love a mountain guide. You have made us the luckiest men in the world.

PREFACE

Just stop for a minute and close your eyes; now imagine that you are standing 14,179 feet above sea level gazing out over much of Northern California. If it is a thought that has crossed your mind, reading this book can turn your thoughts into reality. This book is written and designed specifically for those of you who are motivated to climb Mt. Shasta for the first time using the Avalanche Gulch route. Even if you do not climb the mountain, it is written in such a way that you can sit home in your chair and imagine you are climbing to the summit.

You will be exposed to the hazards and rewards of mountaineering on Mt. Shasta and it will also allow those of you who know little about the mountain to become better acquainted with it. Your journey to the summit will take you up the mountain through the wide-open bowl of Avalanche Gulch on Mt. Shasta's southwest slope. The route is also known as the John Muir/traditional route, the main route, or just Avy Gulch. There are other established routes on the mountain, five of which are also covered in this book; however, Avalanche Gulch is the most popular route taken by novice climbers. On an average, there are currently more than 5,000- 6,000 people annually who attempt to reach the mountain's summit with only about 45% making it.

Our purpose in writing this book is to share our knowledge with novice climbers so they can have a safe, rewarding, and successful climb to Mt. Shasta's summit. All the photographs in this book are taken by SWS Mountain Guides or Steve Lewis from our many climbs to the summit. Throughout the book the word "summit" appears many times. Summit has two meanings: one is the Summit of Mt. Shasta and will always be capitalized, and the other is what climbers refer to as "summit," meaning the act of climbing to the Summit.

CONTENTS

THE MOUNTAIN

Snowcapped Mt. Shasta in all its grandeur towering high in the blue sky stands alone and massive in size, isolating itself

from the rugged peaks that surround it like a lonely pyramid in the desert. The southerly approach up the Sacramento River Canyon, on a winding stretch of Interstate 5, offers tantalizing glimpses through the gaps in the canyon's walls, and then

Aerial View Mt. Shasta Courtesy of USGS

suddenly the mountain materializes into full view as you drive up from the canyon floor.

California's Sacramento Valley begins 60 miles south of Mt. Shasta and stretches down the state until it merges with the San Joaquin Valley. Before the days of automobiles and highways, the pioneers traveled to Mt. Shasta either on foot or horseback. John Muir, nature writer and avid outdoorsman, spent a lot of time in the late 1800s exploring beautiful Mt. Shasta and its surrounding area. The following quotation describes how he felt and what he saw when he had his first glimpse of Mt. Shasta in 1874.

> *"When I first caught sight of it [Mount Shasta] over the braided folds of the Sacramento Valley I was fifty miles away and afoot, alone and weary. Yet all my blood turned to wine, and I have not been weary since."* ......John Muir.....

GEOGRAPHY

Located in the upper regions of northern California, Mt. Shasta is a massive, white giant standing 14,179 feet (4,322 m) above sea level. It is a stratum volcano, a dominant feature of Northern California, and is situated in the largest zone of volcanoes in the world called the Pacific Ring of Fire. Seventy-five percent of the world's volcanoes lie along this ring, which stretches from Alaska to South America and circles the Pacific Ocean,

Mount Shasta's Location in Northern California

heading north through Japan and circling back to Alaska. Mt. Shasta is in a section of this ring called the Cascade Volcanic Arc, which begins 75 miles south of Mt. Shasta in the vicinity of Mt. Lassen (10, 462 ft.), the southernmost peak in the Cascade Range. The Cascade Range extends about 700 miles north from this point through Oregon and Washington into southern British Columbia. There are a total of eighteen major volcanoes in the Cascade Range with elevations ranging from 9,500 feet to a towering height of more than 14,000 feet. Mt. Rainier, in the state of Washington, is the tallest and stands at an elevation of

14,411 feet. Mt. Shasta, the second tallest volcano in the lower 48 states, is 232 feet lower than Rainier, yet more massive.

ERUPTIONS

The last known eruption on Mt. Shasta occurred in 1786 and is reported to have been observed from the Pacific Ocean by a French sea captain named Jean de La Pérouse. Captain de La Pérouse noted seeing a furious fire emanating from the

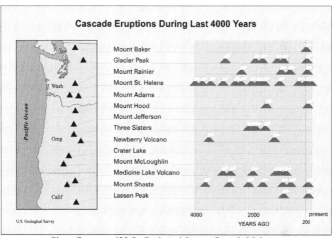

Chart Courtesy of U.S. Geological Survey Cascade Volcanoes

night sky in the direction of Mt. Shasta. His sighting was not proven at the time; however, it was recorded in the ship's log book and eventually sent to France for publication. According to the U.S. Geological Survey, recent geologic studies have shown radiocarbon and geological evidence that an eruption did occur about 200 years ago. Although it has seen almost as much volcanic action as Mt. Saint Helens, it's hard to tell, since Shasta's lower slopes have been covered by a green, coniferous forest in the last 200 years. Mt. Lassen to the south and Mt. Saint Helens to the north have both erupted in this century.

 Mt. Shasta has erupted on average at least once per every 800 years during the past 10,000 years, about once per every 300 years in the past 3,500 years, and about once per every 250 years in the past 750 years indicating that eruptions are becoming more frequent. If the Mountain erupted today, it would leave not only widespread destruction to the local area, but it would dramatically change the nature of the Mt. Shasta area.

On the western flank of Shasta's slopes is the satellite peak of Shastina (12,330 ft.) which topped by a bowl-shaped crater 300 feet deep and one-half mile in diameter. The crater's rim would almost be a complete circle except for the immense rift on its western side. This deep-seated, V-shaped gully is known as Diller Canyon, named by C. H. Merriam, in honor of J. S. Diller, who published the first physiographic account of the mountain in 1885. Shastina is one of Mt. Shasta's vents and is considered to be capable of erupting with greater force than Shasta's main Summit. Shastina's summit pinnacle, located to the south side within the bowl, stands at an elevation of 12,330 feet. Three major vents, as well as many smaller ones are on the mountain, including the Hotlum vent with its Hot Sulphur Springs on Shasta's Summit which serves to remind us that the volcano is indeed still active!

GLACIERS

Mt. Shasta holds eight glaciers on its slopes, which you can see best from certain vantage points during the summer and

First Ice Fall Hotlum Glacier

fall months. Some of the mountain's glaciers can be observed from the valleys below, but the best views, of course, are from the Summit or, better yet, from climbing on one. When the glaciers are free of snow, they are a very spectacular light-blue or sometimes dark-blue in color.

The Whitney Glacier (named after Prof. J. D. Whitney, leader of a famed survey and scientific exploration) is the most massive and longest glacier on the mountain as well as the largest in the state of California. The Whitney Glacier begins just below the saddle between the West Face and Misery Hill, winds down the northwest slope of Shasta to the east side of the saddle, and continues down the north east side of Shastina's slopes. A spectacular view of the Whitney Glacier can be seen from the Summit Plateau and from the north end of the Summit pinnacle. Shasta's two next largest glaciers, the Hotlum (Hot Rock), and Bolam (The Great One), on the mountain's northern slopes can be seen from the Summit itself.

The sixth largest glacier, the Chicago, has been newly named by the University of Chicago because of their recent studies conducted on Mt. Shasta's glaciers. In 2002, scientists made the first detailed study of Mount Shasta's glaciers in 50 years. They found that seven (now eight) of the glaciers have

grown over the period of 1951-2002, with the Hotlum and Wintun nearly doubling, the Bolum increasing by half, and the Whitney and Konwakiton Glaciers by a

Climber ascending the Whitney Glacier

third. Consequently, the Chicago Glacier (formally a section of the Hotlum Glacier) is a recent separation from the Hotlum Glacier adding the eighth glacier to Mt. Shasta flanks. On the eastern slopes is the mountain's fourth largest glacier, the Wintun (a local Indian Tribe), which can also be seen from the Summit.

Although there are no glaciers to cross along the Avalanche Gulch route, your best view of the fifth largest glacier, the Konwakiton (a local Indian name for muddy), is on the east side of the Red Banks at 12,800 feet. The seventh largest glacier, the Mud Creek Glacier, formerly part of Konwakiton, can be partially viewed from a distance while you're standing on the Summit Plateau, but its best view is from Thumb Rock at the top of Sargents Ridge. The smallest of the eight, Watkins Glacier (named after Harry Watkins a local climber who studied the glacier), is tucked away below a sharp ridge on the southeast side of the mountain and is mostly visible from Wintun Ridge or from the Clear Creek route.

FAUNA

Black bears *Ursus Americanus*, are the only bears native to the Mt. Shasta area and can occasionally be seen around the trailheads and lower flanks of the mountain. There has been one recent documented sighting of a black bear as high as Helen Lake, but it is extremely rare to ever see a bear that far above tree line.

While hiking below timberline you may encounter black-

tailed jack rabbits, coyotes, foxes, pine martins, or maybe even a mule deer. Up to timberline you may encounter golden mantle squirrels living in the forest with their cousin, the western chipmunk, locally known as the yellow-pine chipmunk. The chipmunks on Mt. Shasta have black and white pinstripes running

Golden Mantle Ground Squirrel

down their back. They make their home up to an elevation of at least 12,000 feet where you can see them running in high gear looking for food. Occasionally a mule deer or snowshoe hare may venture above timberline.

BIRDS

Mt. Shasta is home to numerous species of birds. Some settle in for a summer home and others like the sparrows and warblers nest year round. While you're hiking the trail to Horse Camp, listen closely and you may hear the hairy and white-headed woodpeckers hammering on Shasta's fir trees.

The woods are full of sounds, such as the mountain Chickadee whistling "*chick-a-dee*" to its mate and the great horned owl bellowing out in the night. You may have to crouch down while the gray jays come swooping over your head. The gray jay, formerly known as the Canada jay and commonly known as *Whiskey Jack* or *Camp Robber*, has a fat, white belly, a white forehead and face, and a back and tail of dark gray. These aggressive birds will fly within inches of your ears and sometimes try to perch on your shoulders. The less aggressive Steller's jay with its brilliant blue body and charcoal-colored head can be easily seen flying through the tree tops. They have sinister looking dark eyes, a sharp pointed beak, and are the only Western jays with a crest.

At timberline the Cassin's finch can be seen flying around the Sierra Club Foundation's cabin. Above timberline, the numerous, crow-sized Clark nutcrackers rule the land around the Whitebark pines. These birds are light gray with black-and-white wings and tail and are white from forehead to breast. Their long, sharply pointed beak resembles the front fang of a crampon and they are often seen tearing open pinecones for seeds. High in the sky, usually soaring above the ridge tops, you may see some hungry Red-tailed, Sharp-shinned, or Cooper's Hawks flaunting their majestic wingspans while looking for a meal below. In the summer you may hear the buzz of a giant bee, but when you turn your head and cringe, you will see that it's just Anna's or Rufous hummingbirds looking for some nectar.

The most enthusiastic birds on the mountain are the Gray-crowned Rosy finches that make high snowfields their home. They feed on the bugs and insects they find lying on the snowfields and in rock crevices. You will find the finches like to spend much of their time walking around your camp searching for food; so make sure you keep your tent zipped because your newly acquired friends may stop in for lunch. Wild birds and animals should not be hand fed because they become too dependent on your generosity. Moreover, on Shasta you will find that the birds have plenty to eat from the flying bugs and seeds. A more recent occurrence over the last few years has been the appearance of ravens up on the mountain especially in the areas where climbers are camping. You have to really keep an eye out for these birds especially if you leave your food out or even bury it in the snow. These birds have become very proficient at digging up food that has been cached in the snow!! Please store your food properly so as to discourage this activity.

FLORA

Mt. Shasta is the second most southerly mountain in the Cascade Range and acts like a divide between northeastern and northwestern California. The Pacific jet stream typically sits over the states of Washington and northern Oregon, causing more precipitation and cooler temperatures to encompass the volcanoes in the Northern Cascades. During the winter months, the jet stream broadens and shifts south over Mt. Shasta, sometimes sending the bulk of the storms through Northern California.

The movement of the jet stream causes the area around Mt. Shasta to have long, hot summers and cold, wet winters which play a vital role in the growth of the flora on Mt. Shasta. There are abundant species of trees, shrubs, and wildflowers that make dramatic changes with the increase of elevation and their location on the mountain.

While traveling up the Everitt Memorial Highway, you can observe some of the more common types of conifers: ponderosa, knob cone, and sugar pine. You may discover a few stands of lodgepole pines, but you will find that they grow mainly on the north and east side of the mountain. However, as you would expect, you will find the Douglas fir and white fir to be the most common species of trees, with

Shasta's Red Fir

some Western (Red) cedar mixed in. Below the 2-mile marker, at 4,000 feet, you will encounter the California Black oak with its sweeping limbs and bright green leaves. Above the 9- marker, at 6,260 feet, you will come upon a grove of California Shasta Red firs in an area now called Red Fir Flat. You will find this particular tree growing only on Mt. Shasta, although there is a similar species of Red fir growing in the southern Sierras. In the late 1800s, John Gill Lemmon, a well known California botanist who spent time on Mt. Shasta, scientifically named the variety of Red fir known as Shasta Red fir.

From the Bunny Flat parking lot (Mile 11), at an elevation of 6,860 feet, to the timberline at 8,000 feet, you will not see any pines, cedars, or Douglas firs, but instead you will notice that the Shasta Red fir and the mountain hemlock dominate the landscape. Also, at the timberline you will discover the tall trees starting to thin, being replaced by thickets of dwarfed white bark pines, commonly called *krummholz (twisted wood)*. You can't miss spotting this twisted looking entanglement that grows up to an elevation of 9,500 feet.

WILDFLOWERS

Several species of plants, flowers, and shrubs grow on the slopes of Mt. Shasta. The most dominant of the shrubs is the Greenleaf Manzanita bush which grows everywhere around the mountain, thinning around the timberline area. Buckbrush, antelope brush, and other chaparral shrubs cover the country side but start to thin out at 7,000 feet, leaving some scattered shrubs up to the timberline. Panther Meadows, at 7,500 feet, holds the *Lilium washingtonianum ssp. purpurascers*, locally known as the Shasta lily, a rare and beautiful flowering plant which comes immediately alive after the snow melts from the edges of the meadows. Panther Meadows is not on the Avalanche Gulch route, but it is well worth a side trip the day before you climb.

Above timberline, the summer wildflowers grow up through the rocks and on the snow's melting edge. The most radiant of the wildflowers are the western paintbrush, locally referred to as Indian paintbrush and the *Pensteman newberryi*, locally known as Pride-of-the-Mountain. Some of the more common of the fragile wildflowers are the alpine buckwheat, Douglas phlox, and the northern mountain laurel, locally known as red heather. Pine lupine, locally known as Shasta lupine, with its white to purple-tinted flower can be seen up to an elevation of 8,500 feet. The Indians would gather its leaves and flowers in the spring. The leaves were steamed and the pea-like flowers

Shasta's Jacob's Ladder

were eaten with acorn soup. Above 13,000 feet, a hardy, but beautiful, white-blossomed flower called the Shasta Jacob's ladder, botanically known as *Polemonium pulcherrimum*, grows alone in the cold, shaded, rocky crevices. When you're hiking off the trails try to avoid crushing these delicate wildflowers with your big mountaineering boots.

MYSTICAL, SACRED, & COMPELLING MOUNT SHASTA

There have been many quotations by early day pioneers who

have felt compelled to express their feelings about Mt. Shasta. Nearly everyone, past and present, appears to be overcome when they see Mt. Shasta because of the mysterious and powerful energy that seems to radiate from the peak. Almost everyone who spends time on

Mystical Mt. Shasta

Mt. Shasta feels the urge to talk of its grandeur, write about its energy, or just spend time on the mountain enjoying Mt. Shasta's intoxicating power and energy.

Mt. Shasta is considered by many to be one of the seven sacred or holy mountains in the world. Sacred mountains like Mt. Fuji in Japan, Mt. Kilimanjaro in Africa, Mt. Kailash in Tibet, and Mt. Shasta are singled out from some of the world's greatest sacred peaks. Sacred mountains like Mt. Shasta have a compelling force that attracts people when they get near these mystical giants. Mt. Shasta has drawn scientists, geologists, meteorologists, naturalists, explorers and just about every other type of person you can imagine. The local Native Americans worship Mt. Shasta as a physical representation of their Creator. *The Creator reached the world below by creating the mountain. He first pushed down the snow and ice from the skies through a hole in the blue heavens and turned a stone round and round till he made this great mountain. The story goes on. He created some more land and seas, and then he built a fire in the center of Mt. Shasta, making the Mountain his home forever after. Once the Creator had finished the world, he sat high on the Mountain and watched to see if what he placed on the earth was to his satisfaction. Later, his family (the ancestors of the present Indians) came down and they lived on the lower slopes of the Mountain.*

The Indians have a term they use in reference to telling their legends, "Yease Nicopesh," meaning "The truth and nothing but the truth." The Indian storyteller was required to repeat these legends orally; to deviate in any form was strictly forbidden. Mt. Shasta to the Indians is beyond churches, beyond temples; it is the Most Holy of Holies. The Indians will not ascend above timberline, not out of fear, but out of respect for the Creator. The only exception to the rule was when an Indian was called to ascend the mountain to die; this was a great honor. In the modern world, many Native Americans feel painfully scorned by the activity that takes place on Mt. Shasta. They feel as though their Creator is being desecrated and that everybody disregards their beliefs.

"At last the water went down. . . . Then the animal people came down from the top of Mount Shasta and made new homes for themselves. They scattered everywhere and became the ancestors of all the animal peoples of the earth." Shasta Indian Flood Legend.

Mt. Shasta is a mountain of mystery with its legends, mythology, and folklore. The most famous of which may be the legend of the Lemurians whom many believe inhabit Mt. Shasta. It is believed that this elusive super race belongs to what was once part of the lost continent of Lemuria (Mu) and Mt. Shasta was the highest point on their eastern coast. Because of natural disasters long ago, the vast continent of Mu submerged and the Lemurians fled to higher ground for safety.

Mythically speaking, there is a golden city inside Mt. Shasta named Telos. The city is said to be built inside an artificial dome-shaped cavern in the Earth a mile or so beneath the mountain. There are conflicting stories about who reside within the golden city, but it is believed the Lemurians are the inhabitants.

The legend also tells about certain unusual bells found on the slopes of Mt. Shasta and within the mass of the peak itself. The bells were made by a race of beings called the Secret Commonwealth who reside in the magnificent cities of Ilethelem and Yaktayvia somewhere beneath Mt. Shasta. These Yaktayvians were reputed to be the greatest bell makers in the world. Supposedly, their underground cities beneath Mt. Shasta were built with the sound of their bells and mighty chimes which moved enormous masses of debris and rocks. The continuous sounds of the bells also illuminate the great halls, corridors and tunnels in the city by vibrating atoms to produce light.

The entrance to the underground world is said to be located on the northwest side of the peak where there is supposedly a great transparent bell that reflects light. When the wind strikes the lip of the bell, a mysterious high-pitched sound instantly frightens any invaders away from the entrance. For others, Mt. Shasta is believed to be a point of cosmic power. The strange lenticular clouds that sometimes appear on the mountain are a phenomenon that is believed by some to be related to the arrival and departure of Unidentified Flying Objects. Supposedly, the top of the mountain opens up and the space craft descends for a pit stop at their fueling station. Stories of UFOs date way back. Some people have reported and written about the strange lights and spaceships they've seen emanating from Mt. Shasta.

PEACEFUL MOUNT SHASTA

The spiritual appeal of Mt. Shasta has attracted many psychics, mystics, and New Age believers to move into the area. There are a large number of religious groups and various organizations who live on or near the mountain and consider it a shrine. Sometimes people who live across the country or just a few miles away have been compelled to be at the mountain just for nourishment of their spirit. They come from all over the world to attend workshops, performances, gatherings, or some just come to spend time on the mountain praying or meditating. There is another group of people who come to Mt. Shasta, but they come to fish, hunt, swim, hike, ski, climb, or relax in the outdoors.

Mt. Shasta and the surrounding area have so much to offer that it's hard to leave it, and some of us don't. Almost everyone is seeking relief from the pressures and hassles of the normal daily grind. Whenever we are of troubled mind or spirit we should think of going to the mountains. Once we are there, we will find ourselves being renewed in spirit and passion toward life. We can all benefit from the peace and solitude found on beautiful Mt. Shasta as long as we respect

ourselves and each other and treat the mountain as a true gift
for ourselves and the generations to follow.

A cosmic, lenticular cloud engulfs the summit of Mt. Shasta

*"Through numbing blizzards or the softness of a summer evening,
never give up holding gratitude for a Mountain as powerful, and giving
as Shasta; you can never be too humble for her."*
Robert Webb, 1996,
Caretaker Sierra Club Foundation's Cabin (Horse Camp)

CLIMBING

WHY WE CLIMB

"I appreciate why I come to the mountains; not to conquer them but to immerse myself in their incomprehensible immensity—so much bigger than we are; to better comprehend humility and patience balanced in harmony, with the desire to push hard . . . and to share it in the long run with my friends . . . and with my own sons."
Alex Lowe

"Mountain climbing is extended periods of intense boredom interrupted by occasional moments of sheer terror."
Anonymous

Climbing a majestic volcano like Mt. Shasta will test your endurance beyond your imagination. So why would you subject yourself to undue risks and danger? Why would you battle the cold, fight the wind, risk a severe sunburn or blisters on your feet, all the while struggling with a 40-50 pound pack on your back, trying to get to a place that you may spend but a few precious moments? Why would you push when your body has already been pushed way beyond its limits?

The answer, as you might imagine, is multidimensional and extremely difficult to articulate. As a matter of fact, many of us cannot really put words to it at all. For many who spend time on the mountain there is no way to convey to our satisfaction why we climb. If we were able to put it into words, the resulting answer would no doubt include the following terms: achievement, character building, and spiritual self-realization. We climb to achieve something great. To challenge ourselves beyond what we think we might be capable of and as a result better ourselves. If climbing a mountain were easy, why would we do it? Success in our day to day lives does not come easy! Perhaps by climbing a mountain we reaffirm this fact. The answer will be different for each and every one of us, and therefore the only way to find your answer is to get out there and climb that mountain.

"Climbing to me is moving meditation. When I am up high on a sheet of ice, nothing else exists except for what is right there in front of me. My world consists of my pounding heart, frozen fingers and toes, laboring lungs, aching legs, the crunch of my crampons as they bite the ice, the thwack of my ice tools as they dig into the frozen water, and my frozen breath. All worries such as work, school, bills, and life just retreat into the background. All thought just ceases to exist. I am existing… in the moment."
David Cressman Co-Owner SWS Mountain Guides

MENTAL PREPARATION

Mountaineers say the greatest obstacle to success is your mental attitude. You may be in great physical shape, but it won't get you to the Summit without having a positive attitude and firm commitment. Reaching your goal and returning safely must be foremost on your mind, and this requires constant focus of mind and body. Most climbers who do not reach the Summit usually turn back because of their attitude and lack of preparation, not the altitude.

The hardships and rewards are awaiting you on the mountain whether it is your first time climbing or one hundredth. Every time you climb your experience will be unique because of the ever changing forces of nature, the varying conditions you can encounter, as well as your mental and physical shape. Having a good positive attitude allows you to face the challenges you seek, treat the mountain with respect, and remember it's not the Summit which is important, but the journey that is traveled. If for some reason you fail in your attempt to reach your goal, remember that the mountain will always be there for you to climb another day.

PHYSICAL PREPARATION

Over many years of guiding people of all ages and ability levels the one thing that has become evident is that people generally do not arrive at Mt. Shasta in good enough physical condition. Remember that even the easiest route on the mountain requires rigorous physical training. If there were only one piece of advice that one could give it would be not to train just to climb the mountain but rather train to enjoy the climb. That is to say that you want to be in good enough shape physically that you can take the mountain at your own pace and not have to suffer through the experience.

There are many books available in the stores and online with regards to physical training and diet and each person should try and find the training regimen that works best for him or her, but here we have outlined our tips to physical preparedness with regards to mountaineering.

1) Focus on cardiovascular strength. This seems to be the greatest area of weakness amongst most beginning mountaineers. So often people find themselves short of breath leading to the Summit that it makes the experience of summiting difficult and unpleasant.

2) Muscle endurance. Mountaineering can be a long all day affair and your legs are the muscle group used for the ascension of any mountain.

Working your legs and core (stomach and back) for endurance, with lots of reps with low weight is preferred.

3) Find a training regimen that you enjoy. If you don't find your workout engaging then find a new way to train. Otherwise you will get bored and you will not continue on your training cycle. Feel free to mix it up to keep up your interest, run, bike, swim, walk, hike, ski and climb, any type of cardiovascular training is great but you have to do it on a regular basis.

4) Set a goal. Set a hiking or climbing objective and a date, then stay focused on that goal throughout your training.

SAMPLE TRAINING SCHEDULE

Train at least 4-5 times per week for at least 40-60 minutes each session in one of the following categories or a mixture of each: running, bicycling, swimming, stair or elliptical machines. Include in your workout some type of flexibility training 3 times a week (stretching for at least 10 minutes). Your workout plans should include at least a couple 2-4 hour weekend training hikes or climbs with your loaded pack (30-40 lbs) for overall conditioning and fitness. Running or walking stairs or stadium bleachers is an excellent training option for mountaineering as well.

One of the best ways to get in shape for any sport is to participate in that sport. To condition yourself for climbing Mt. Shasta, you may find it beneficial to take day hikes to Helen Lake at 10,443 feet, or better yet, take a strenuous climb to one of the ridge tops. Another great option is to complete a series of intense training hikes on your local hill or mountain. We suggest to our clients carrying a weighted pack filled with a couple liters of water (2.2 lbs per liter) and emptying the bottles at the summit. This is a great way to save your knees on the descent during those training hikes. You should train for the climb as you would for any other strenuous sport by pushing your limits and training hard!

WARNING: <u>Before embarking on any exercise or conditioning programs, please consult your physician.</u>

CLIMBING SKILLS DEVELOPMENT

There are some basic mountaineering skills that must be learned before attempting to climb Mt. Shasta. Two of the more important of these skills is the use of the ice axe and crampons. Going into these in depth is beyond the scope of this book, but the easiest way to learn these skills is to take a relatively inexpensive, one day ice axe/crampon clinic. This clinic will get you acquainted with the use of climbing equipment and with crossing moderate to steep snowfields. Taking the course held on Mt. Shasta has a special advantage since the instructors are familiar with the mountain's routes, conditions, and weather. You will then have a golden opportunity to ask the experts your questions and obtain all the information that you will need. The course should also give you some idea as to what type of physical hardships you will encounter. In our clinics we cover a variety of topics including, pressure breathing, self-care at high altitudes, the different stepping techniques, pacing, and glissading.

THE FIRST RECORDED CLIMB

The first recorded Summit ascent of Mt. Shasta dates back to the mid-1800s. Captain Elias D. Pierce is credited with the first ascent on Mt. Shasta on August 14, 1854. His climb to the Summit, with a party of eight, required the courage and skill of a mountain climber. According to *The Pierce Chronicle*, he describes part of their trip as follows:

"With muffled boots, hatchet in hand and a rope securely attached around my waist, the rope slackened in the hands of those who remained behind, I launched out still in a meeke position, chipping out steps as I advanced, a distance of about sixty feet. Safely across, I called to the men to keep their courage. They came, one at a time, till all were over and looking back on our ice stair way it was a frightful to think of ever trying to make the descent that way. In climbing from one cliff to another, had we made one misstep, we would have gone headlong over a perpendicular precipice a thousand feet to the base."

Before Pierce's ascent, the general population living around the Mt. Shasta area thought climbing to Mt. Shasta's Summit was impossible. To prove the skeptics and disbelievers wrong and to legitimatize his earlier feat, Pierce made a second ascent on September 19, 1854. This time he took nine climbers with him, and one was a writer from Scott Valley named John Mckee. According to *The Pierce Chronicle,* Pierce said while standing on the Summit:

"All the scenery beneath was the most beautiful that my eyes ever looked upon. About 2 o'clock P. M. we planted the Stars and Stripes on the Summit of Shasta Butte; and after lettering the face of a smooth, flat stone with a cold-chisel the year, day, and date, we left the flag floating in the breeze, and began the descent on the same route as far as the snow plane. From that point we explored a new route farther to the

south and found it to be much the best. We came to a point that we gave the name of Red Bluff."

We can assume that Pierce's new route was the Avalanche Gulch route and the "Red Bluffs" are referred to today as the Red Banks. Pierce continued to climb Mt. Shasta in the years to follow, setting an example for others.

WHEN TO GO

The climbing season on Mt. Shasta is from mid-May to early September, a relatively long season for a Cascade peak. Usually, the best times to climb are from early-June through late July depending on yearly snow conditions. The snow conditions are more preferable and the weather is generally more stable during these months. Early in the climbing season you can have winter like conditions with late spring storms and avalanche conditions can persist. Late in the climbing season when the snow is apt to be patchy or gone, the loose ash and rocky volcanic soil does not provide solid footing, and the danger of rock fall increases. Holidays on the popular routes such as Avalanche Gulch are usually crowded, so if you are looking for solitude then you may want to pick a non-holiday weekend, a mid-week climb, or try one of the less crowded routes such as Clear Creek or Hotlum/Bolum Ridge. Most beginner climbers choose to go up during the summer while some of the more experienced mountaineers, looking for an added challenge, attempt winter ascents using the Casaval Ridge or Sargent's Ridge routes to avoid obvious avalanche hazards in Avalanche Gulch during the winter season.

The Avalanche Gulch and the Clear Creek routes are the "easiest" to follow, however, the Clear Creek route, located on the southeast slope, is accessible only in the summer by dirt road. Although the word "easy" is used among climbers, these routes are far from being easy. There are no easy routes on Mt. Shasta, just different ones! Both routes are generally suitable for the inexperienced climber, however, the Avalanche Gulch route is recommended for the first-time climber since there will almost always be someone on the route. Traveling the Clear Creek route is actually safer with less rock fall danger, but you may not see another person on the route until you reach the Summit. We discourage beginner climbers from climbing by themselves. It is best to join a group of more experienced climbers.

The best time for skiing and snowboarding from the Summit is early May through mid June. Ski mountaineering does continue late into the season (late June through July) on the North and East sides of Mt. Shasta, as long as the snow conditions stay consistent and the dreaded sun cups have not formed. The North and Eastside routes will stay skiable longer because they receive much less direct sunlight early in the year. The usual time frame for skiing these routes is dictated by when the Northgate and Brewer Creek trailheads open. In a lighter snow year these trailheads may open by early June but in a heavy snow year may not be open till mid June to early July.

CLIMBING DISTANCE AND TIME

The hiking distance from Bunny Flat to the Summit is about six uphill miles, with an elevation gain of more than 7,000 feet. How long it takes you to climb to the Summit depends on your physical conditioning, the snow conditions, and how many days you allow to reach the Summit. Some people assume the Mountain can be climbed in one day and it is possible, however, you had better be in pretty darn good physical shape and have already become accustomed to high altitudes. One-day climbs average about 15 hours with most of the time for the ascent. Although the trip can be done in one day, we strongly suggest, especially for the inexperienced climber, that you take two to three days and make an overnight base camp at Helen Lake (10,400 feet), 50/50 Flat (9,200 feet), or Horse Camp (8,000 feet).

The average climbing time for the first day is about 4-7 hours from the Bunny Flat parking lot to Helen Lake and that is while carrying a full pack. If you leave the parking lot early in the morning, you should arrive at Helen Lake around noon. The second day requires a lot more time because you will be climbing from Helen Lake to the Summit, back to Helen Lake, and then making the final descent to the parking lot. Average climbing time from Helen Lake to the Red Banks is about 2-4 hours, and from there to the Summit about 2-4 more hours.

Descending time from the Summit back to Helen Lake takes about 2-4 hours, depending on the snow conditions. From Helen Lake to the parking lot averages 3 hours hiking time. Climbing times do vary. The snow conditions are constantly changing on the mountain and your climbing times can change as well. You also need to consider time for breaks, pondering over the views, and chatting with other climbers. Your second day should be judged by the amount of daylight you have, so take care to not let yourself get caught in the dark on the way back to the parking lot. Getting a very early start on your Summit day is mandatory. Leaving Helen Lake between 2-4 am is not unwarranted!

SPECIAL EQUIPMENT

Ice Screws are needed on Mt. Shasta's Glaciers.

The equipment you need depends on the route you select and the time of year you choose to climb. **On every route, however, you MUST have an ice axe, a helmet, and crampons.** Other equipment such as ropes, snow/ice anchors, and belay devices are necessary on some of the more technical routes. The novice climber must spend many hours learning the proper use of equipment before attempting any serious climbing on Mt. Shasta. On Avalanche Gulch, you may need snowshoes and you definitely will need a snow shovel during the early climbing season and sometimes even during the summer months. Ski poles are very helpful for stabilization when carrying a full pack and we highly suggest using a pair. Good quality gear and the knowledge on how to properly use it will allow for a safer and more comfortable climb. For a full discussion of the gear and equipment requirements, see the Climbing Gear Chapter starting on page 56.

CLIMBING WEATHER

The weather on Mt. Shasta is the most important factor in planning your trip. Inclement weather is one of the largest contributors to injury or death on Mt Shasta and should be taken very seriously. Even when temperatures are warm and winds are calm at the trailhead, the weather higher up on the mountain can often include subzero temps and hurricane force winds. Climbing up into unstable weather conditions should not be attempted unless you are a well-seasoned, experienced climber who is very familiar with the route and is aware of the hazards and risks of mountain weather.

GUIDE SERVICES

The services of professional guide companies are increasing in popularity on Mt. Shasta for both guided climbs and educational courses. These courses can range from beginner, one-day ice axe clinics and introductory guided climbs to advanced, weeklong seminars on ski mountaineering or Denali/Himalayan preparation courses on Mt. Shasta's glaciers. SWS Mountain Guides is one of the three insured permitted operators on Mt. Shasta; all others work through these 3 permitted companies. A full list of the permitted operators is available on the U.S. Forest Service website listed in Appendix A.

PERMITS

You must have a wilderness permit before climbing the mountain or entering the Mt. Shasta Wilderness Area. All of the area above 8,000 feet and some of the areas below timberline are located within the Mt. Shasta Wilderness Area. There are no quotas on the number of permits available; however you are required to have a wilderness permit. Permits are currently free for camping in the Wilderness Area and are issued from the Mt. Shasta and McCloud Forest Service offices as well as the main trailheads. Campfire permits are also required for anyone having an open fire underline the Wilderness Area and within the National Forest and can be obtained at the Mt. Shasta Ranger Station. During the winter it is best to obtain your wilderness permit in advance at the Mt. Shasta Ranger Station because the trailheads may be snowed in.

Restrictions have been placed in the Mt. Shasta Wilderness Area and on some visitor activities that create the greatest impacts to the wilderness ecosystem. Included among these regulations is a limit on party size (the maximum is 10 people) and on the length of stay in the Wilderness Area (7 nights). Now in effect is a prohibition on dogs and wood campfires. In addition, visitors are asked to stay on designated trails in the spring-fed meadows and to confine all camping, washing, and depositing of bodily wastes to areas at least 200 feet, or more, from streams, springs, trails, and camps. Before leaving home, you should check with the Mt. Shasta Ranger Station to find out what other restrictions may be applicable to your specific recreation plans.

The permit system allows the Wilderness Rangers to keep a database on the number of people using the Mountain and/or the Wilderness Area. Every five years, any ranger station having a Wilderness Area within its National Forest boundary is required to make an assessment of its usage. Filling out a permit also makes funding easier to obtain in the event improvements are needed within the area. Currently a climber's board, located outside the main entrance to the Mt. Shasta Ranger Station, contains information and instructions about the regulations on Mt. Shasta and within the Wilderness Area.

There is currently health, aesthetic, and environmental problems associated with the disposal of human waste (feces) on climbing routes in the Mt. Shasta Wilderness. Helen Lake on the Avalanche Gulch route is the worst area on the Mountain for this problem. Climbers and Wilderness Rangers have developed a mandatory Human Waste Packout System in an effort to decrease such problems. You can obtain the human-waste kits with instructions at the Mt. Shasta Ranger Station or at any of the trailheads. Currently the Forest Service provides the waste-kits free of charge and all climbers are required to use them.

Approximately 7,000 wilderness (visitors) permits are filled out annually with about 5,400 of these people having attempted to reach the Mt. Shasta's Summit with only about 45% making it. In addition to the Wilderness permit a <u>Mt. Shasta Summit Pass</u> is required for anyone climbing to the Summit, or above 10,000 feet, or their intent is to attain the Summit. As of the printing of this book, the cost for a Summit Pass is $20.00 per person and it is good for three days from the date of purchase. You can also take advantage of the Annual Pass for only $30.00. You should check with the Mt. Shasta Ranger Station for any changes in the permit requirements.

MOUNT SHASTA'S WEATHER

"Climbing on Mt. Shasta will prepare you for any mountain in the world, climb enough on Mt. Shasta and you will encounter every type of extreme weather."
Timothy Keating, SWS Mountain Guides Founder

Weather on any mountain can be unpredictable at times, but nowhere is this truer than in the Cascades. Due to Mt. Shasta's close proximity to the Pacific Ocean, large storms can form very quickly and move in over the mountain with very little warning. This, coupled with the high elevation of

Mt. Shasta sticks up above everything for hundreds of miles.

Mt Shasta, can mean extreme volatility in the weather. During a hot summer day in July, you can be standing in the town of Mount Shasta at 3,536 ft, looking up at the Mountain, and never guess that the temperature on the Summit could be well below freezing. A Summit attempt in the month of August might be marked with sub-freezing temperatures and 60 to 70 mile per hour winds blowing across Misery Hill. In contrast, we have had Summit climbs in January and February where we were descending from the Summit stripped down to short sleeved shirts with not a breath of wind.

The weather conditions on the mountain are constantly changing. The storms that move into Northern California typically come from the west off the Pacific Ocean and can often produce rain and snow at anytime. The precipitation tends to be heaviest on the west, and south sides of the mountain while the east and north sides can receive much less rain or snow. Mt. Shasta is so large in scale it acts like its own mountain range by creating a "rain shadow" effect on the north and eastern slopes.

Some of the winter storms that come plunging down from the Gulf of Alaska are called the "Arctic Express" driven by the jet stream over northern California. Unfortunately, Mt. Shasta, due in part to its high elevation, can be the first mountain that these storms encounter while they track across the continent producing powerful hurricane force winds, cold arctic type temperatures and huge snowfalls. In the winter of 2010, the Avalanche Gulch area had snow depths in excess of 30 feet and hurricane force winds due to the recurrence of these types of storms.

During the summer months, a strong, high pressure usually dominates Northern California, bringing months of good, <u>hot</u>, dry weather, causing most of the snow to rapidly melt off the mountain. This type of weather can make for excellent thunderstorm formation when you add in the acclimated snowpack and the high altitude on Mt. Shasta. These summer thunderstorms can produce severe lightning, heavy rain and sometimes snow on the mountain as well as afternoon downpours in the valleys below. Other times these afternoon build ups of cumulus

Thunder Clouds can form rapidly during the summer months

39

clouds may encompass the mountain and block visibility on the Summit without producing any precipitation. This condition is known as a "white-out" and can leave climbers looking for the route down the mountain.

Additionally, due to the massive evaporation, the up and down drafts associated with this size of a mountain, Mt. Shasta can produce its own weather. When a mild summer storm approaches Mt. Shasta, the clouds can and will form around the mountain, causing severe weather conditions on the peak, while not effecting the valleys or surround plains below

Lenticular clouds are another common phenomenon on Mt. Shasta. These clouds are usually accompanied with high winds, low visibility, and sometimes rain or snow. This mysterious looking, round, white cap is formed when expanding, warm, marine air impacts the cold mountain air

and can occur at anytime. Lenticular clouds come in different sizes and shapes, but generally resembles several flying saucers stacked on top of each other.

Lenticular Cloud formed over Mt. Shasta

This phenomenon is very spectacular if viewed from the valleys below. When lenticular clouds envelope the Mountain it is an indication of a cold and very windy summit If you get caught climbing in one of these clouds; a hasty descent is a must.

Looking down on Thumb Rock as Mt. Shasta is making its own weather.

Several automated weather stations dot the surrounding flanks of Mt. Shasta recording temperature, precipitation wind speed and snow depth. All this information is fed into the central Mount Shasta Ranger Station data base and is used by the Wilderness Rangers to predict weather, avalanche and climbing conditions on Mt. Shasta. Similar sources are used by the National Weather Service otherwise known as NOAA (National Oceanic and Atmospheric Administration) to make weather predictions for Mt. Shasta and the surrounding areas. All this information, reports and weather predictions including the automated weather stations can be accessed via www.shastaavalanche.org Please use this information to make sound judgments on when and where to climb on Mt. Shasta.

MOUNTAIN SAFETY

"Just a reminder – a guidebook is no substitute for skill,
experience, judgment, and lots of tension."
Charlie Fowler

PERSONAL SAFETY

The ascent of Mt. Shasta, as well as many other mountains, can easily be underestimated and is often not taken seriously enough. As a mountaineer, you can often be lulled into a false sense of security by the surreal nature of your surroundings and the recent story of a fellow climber attaining the Summit on a bright, warm, windless day in May in only a t-shirt! Safety must be the first and foremost factor you consider when planning the climb and while climbing the route you have selected. The very nature and lure of mountaineering is the unpredictability of the adventure. Failure to put on your crampons when needed or to heed the warning of avalanches or rock fall danger is not tolerated in the sport of mountaineering with the possible consequences being severe. The mountain is ambivalent in nature so do not under estimate Mt. Shasta or over estimate your skills or experience. As the old saying goes;

"There are old climbers, there are bold climbers,
but no old bold climbers!"
Anonymous

Before you climb any route, you should familiarize yourself with the safety aspects needed for that particular route. For example bowls and open faces tend to lend themselves to avalanche and rock fall danger whereas ridge routes tend to have higher winds and cornice hazards. Glacier routes have unique hazards in the form of crevasses, icefalls and should be traveled with other experienced climbers or with a permitted guide service. This chapter provides an overview of some of the problems related to mountain safety that you are likely to encounter on Mt. Shasta, not a comprehensive list, and not a substitute for proper training and experience. There are multiple incidents every year on Mt. Shasta that result in climbers getting lost, injured, or even killed. There have been times when climbers have become lethargic or even incapacitated because of altitude illness. Normally, accidents happen on the mountain because of a climber's poor judgment, improper mountaineering skills or lack of experience.

You need to be aware of two types of safety hazards that you may encounter when climbing Mt. Shasta. First are the **objective dangers** or the obvious dangers of the mountain's natural hazards such as rock fall, avalanche, and weather related conditions. The second are the **subjective dangers**, which describe your ability to ensure a safe passage by attaining the correct skills, by making the proper choice of quality equipment, and by exercising good judgment while climbing. The chance of getting injured or even losing your life because of poor skills, use of faulty equipment, and bad judgment is always present when you are involved with the sport of climbing. Being aware of all aspects of mountaineering safety will assure you and your group a safe climb to the Summit and return to the trailhead.

You should always keep a constant awareness of what goes on around you and especially if someone is climbing above or below you. There is nothing more hazardous than having another climber above you carelessly kicking rocks down on top of you. The following are some mountaineering hazards that need to be recognized.

ROCK FALL

Due to the porous and brittle nature of volcanic rock on Mt. Shasta rock fall occurs daily somewhere on the mountain. This is especially true below the Red Banks and the Trinity Chutes and the ridges on the east and west where exposed rock hangs over much of the Avalanche Gulch route. It is one of the most common threats you will encounter while climbing Mt Shasta and has injured and killed numerous climbers over the years.

Wearing a climber's helmet is imperative but it is also important to understand their limitations. The best safety precaution that you can take is –to maintain a constant awareness for falling rocks and where your route is in relationship to this hazard. You may notice by early morning the ice on the rock faces above Avalanche Gulch will start to melt. When this happens, the melting ice sometimes will break off in chunks and send small rocks, blocks of ice, or even large boulders showering the gulch with rock and ice debris. Rock fall danger is a serious threat to climbers on Mt. Shasta. Learn how to minimize this danger by wearing a helmet, selecting the right route, and the right time to climb.

AVALANCHES   Know before you go!

"There is a reason it's called Avalanche Gulch."
Norm Wilson – Avalanche Expert

Though most avalanches occur in the winter and spring time or surrounding a recent snow cycle it is imperative to realize that avalanches can occur throughout most of the year on Mt. Shasta given the right conditions. When conditions are questionable it is usually preferable to avoid these risks by

In the late spring, cornices break off Casaval ridge and slide into Avalanche Gulch

attempting to climb via one of the more technical ridge routes rather than the open faces or gulches that lend themselves to becoming terrain traps. Obviously if these routes are beyond your skill level then your Summit attempt will have to be postponed!

Avalanche forecasting and climbing advisories are provided through the Mt. Shasta Avalanche Center and the Forest Service. Updated avalanche conditions can be found at the Mt. Shasta Ranger Station or are frequently posted at the local gear shops. You can also find the avalanche forecast online at www.shastaavalanche.org. Please remember that this is just one tool you can use to plan your trip and the advisory is just that, an advisory. It should by no means be the last thing you look at to determine whether it is safe "to go" or "not go" into the backcountry.

It is important for climbers and skiers to not only understand the risks but also the signs of avalanche conditions. It is incumbent on the group to rescue themselves in the event that someone gets caught in a slide. If you are not knowledgeable about avalanches, courses and education are offered throughout the winter by the local guiding services.

HYPOTHERMIA

Cold weather, especially if it is combined with rain, snow and wind, can bring about hypothermia, a condition in which the body's core temperature lowers to below normal levels. Hypothermia occurs when the body loses heat at a rate faster than it can be replaced. It is important to note that due to the nature of the weather on Mt Shasta, hypothermia can occur at anytime throughout the year. When it comes to hypothermia the key is prevention. Make sure that you are well equipped with the appropriate clothing and equipment while climbing and camping on Mt. Shasta.

FROSTNIP and FROSTBITE

Frostnip and its more insidious brother frostbite are both conditions defined by the freezing of living tissues. Whereas frostnip is just the freezing of surface tissue, frostbite occurs when the underlying tissues are frozen as well. This is usually most common in exposed skin and in your extremities such as your fingers and toes where circulation tends to be poor and away from the core of the body. It is important to remember that, much like hypothermia, frostbite can occur at almost any time of year on Mt. Shasta. Gloves, thick socks, and complete face protection will diminish your chances of frostbite. It is also important to understand that frostbite is more common at higher elevations due to the reduced oxygen and the colder environment. At higher elevations your body is less efficient at producing internal warmth, making the exposed parts of the body more susceptible to freezing. Direct exposure to extreme cold or high winds causes the extremities to lose heat faster than heat can be replaced by the circulating blood.

ALTITUDE ILLNESSES

Acute Mountain Sickness (AMS) is also sometimes referred to as altitude sickness. The altitude at which AMS can occur is specific both to a person's genetic makeup and their previous acclimatization to altitude. The primary symptoms include; headache, lack of appetite, and fatigue; generally similar to a bad hangover. Additional notable symptoms may also include nausea, vomiting, and lethargy.

Though AMS is linked to dehydration it is important to note that the only treatment for AMS is immediate descent. Although over the counter anti-inflammatory pain medications such as ibuprofen or aspirin may relieve the pain and other symptoms associated with AMS they to do not resolve the underlying cause which is altitude, for which descending is the best treatment. It is imperative when these symptoms do not improve with rest or become increasingly severe that the person begins to **descend** with another climber as soon as possible. Failure to do so could result in the AMS worsening and perhaps progressing into life threatening conditions such as High Altitude Cerebral Edema (HACE) or High Altitude Pulmonary Edema (HAPE).

LIGHTNING

Lightning is a very common occurrence on Mt. Shasta during the summer months, but luckily, one of the less frequent causes of injuries on the mountain. The best way to avoid a lightning storm is to climb early and be descending before the early afternoon thunderstorms develop. Lightning, like all other forms of electricity, will seek the path of least resistance, hitting the highest ground first.

Standing on the Summit or on one of the ridge tops is not the place to be during a lightning storm. A hasty retreat is most advisable.

FIRST AID

A basic knowledge of first aid is helpful not only for yourself but for others as well. There are two main companies that offer first aid certification specific to the wilderness setting: Wilderness Medical Associates (WMA) and Wilderness Medical Institute (WMI). They both offer excellent courses at several levels from basic to advanced wilderness first aid training. Classes last from one day up to four weeks and are offered throughout the country. For additional information and a complete schedule at: www.wildmed.com or www.nols.edu/wmi.

As for First Aid Kits, you can either buy a "readymade" First Aid Kit or put one together yourself (see Appendix D for a list of basic supplies). You should consider the weight and size of your first aid kit and only take what you need for the specific climb that you will be on. Commercially made First Aid Kits range in quality from excellent to not worth carrying. If you decide to purchase a kit we recommend Adventure Medical Kits for their quality, size and weight. (www.adventuremedicalkits.com)

RESCUE

Many accidents and even deaths have taken place on Mt. Shasta since the mountain was first climbed in the 1800's. Rescue efforts on the mountain are done as a collaborative effort between the Forest Service Wilderness Rangers, Guides Services and the Siskiyou County Sheriff's Search and Rescue team. The county SAR is a volunteer crew that is responsible for arranging rescue efforts on the mountain and the surrounding area. The availability of rescue depends on many things such as weather conditions, available manpower, and the availability of helicopters and other equipment.

When an accident does occur, the injured person's partner usually has to signal another climber to look for help. The partner should never leave the injured one unless absolutely necessary. Some climbers carry two-way radios for emergencies, but with today's technology, a cellular phone would be the best safety device that a climber could carry. Cell service is generally pretty good on the south and west sides of Mt. Shasta, but, spotty and dependent on your service provider, on the north and east sides of the peak.

Wilderness Rangers patrolling the mountain in the summer are usually the first ones to be alerted if there is an accident or injury. They do carry two-way radios and can help with coordinating a rescue attempt. The rescued climber is not charged directly for his or her rescue, however, the county in which the rescue took place, which would be Siskiyou County for Mt. Shasta, has the option of billing the county where the rescued person resides. Most rescues involve a helicopter and other equipment along with volunteer manpower which sometimes add up to a very big expense. One exception to the injured party not having to pay for a rescue is when certain helicopters are involved. If the CHP helicopters are involved there is no charge to the injured party, BUT, if other, private, choppers are called in, the injured party could be saddled with bills as high as $25,000!

RESCUE STORY

Several years ago, at 4:45 a.m., Saturday, September 10, an inexperienced climber left the Bunny Flat trailhead headed for a solo attempt on the Summit. He had been told that climbing to the Summit could be done in one day. Furthermore, a fellow local hiker had informed him that because of the unusually dry summer, the Summit could be climbed without the use of crampons or an ice axe, if he followed the usual route.

He started his climb early in the morning with only enough food and water to last him one day. After climbing for several hours, he reached the Red Banks. The weather was deteriorating and the temperature was plunging around him. He did not know that a group of climbers behind him had turned back before the Red Banks because of the bad weather. The solo climber continued until a thick fog moved in, giving way to zero visibility and below freezing temperatures. He set a pile of rocks on top of the snowfield to use as a marker, and then he walked about twenty feet in one direction. Unsure of exactly where he was, he stopped and turned but never again found his rock marker. With snow beginning to fall, he headed back down what he assumed was the Red Banks. He was actually walking the opposite way down the steep, Konwakiton Glacier. After several bad and painful falls, he wound up spending a sleepless night below the Konwakiton Glacier, somewhere on the east slope of Mud Creek Canyon on a small, unstable, shale rock ledge that could barely hold his weight.

He spent the following morning dodging rock fall from above while he slowly climbed back up the canyon. By noon, he had climbed the canyon and was attempting to return to Avalanche Gulch by crossing back over the Red Banks, although he first had to climb up Konwakiton Glacier without an ice axe or crampons. By late Sunday night the fatigued climber, alone and without water or food, had miraculously survived the treacherous climb up the Konwakiton Glacier.

He did have an altimeter with him and became depressed when he realized at 2:00 a.m. on Monday that he was just a few hundred feet below the Summit at 13,800 feet, and not descending the Red Banks at 12,800 feet. Still alive, but severely bruised, he had no choice but to once again bravely face the bitterly cold wind and the possibility of death while he spent another lonely night on one of the mountain's slopes.

Completely lost, frostbitten, and sick to his stomach, he decided after sleeping for 2 hours to try and descend to the Red Banks and Avalanche Gulch. Once again, completely disoriented, the climber made a very costly mistake by descending the steepest side of the Mountain, the northwest side. Having no ice axe, he had no other option but to take the Phillips screwdriver in his Swiss army knife and use the little driver as a miniature ice axe.

The climber, extremely fatigued and hallucinating, realized the only hope of survival was to be rescued. Before the climb, he had instructed his brother that if he did not call by Saturday night at 10:00 p.m., the brother was to call the Ranger Station for help. Two days later on Monday afternoon, the exhausted climber was close to collapsing when he spotted the rescue helicopter flying in the area.

Mud Creek Canyon — the arrow shows approximately where the lost climber spent his first, cold night

The climber was not wearing any brightly colored clothes, and he appeared camouflaged against the dark rocks on the side of the mountain. Unnoticed, he watched the chopper make many passes over him. It was not until the eighth pass that one of the rescue crew members spotted him.

The pilot of the chopper, having nowhere to land, took a chance and situated one wheel close to the ground which allowed two of the rescue crew members to vacate the chopper and assist the needy climber. Because of the high altitude, the chopper could not stay above 13,000 feet for more than an hour. The pilot was forced to descend to a lower elevation until it was safe to return to 13,000 feet where he had left the rescuers and the climber.

The weather, once again, started to deteriorate and the flight was close to being aborted. The rescue crew and climber waited in the cold wind, praying for the return of the chopper. They could hear in the distance the whipping in the air and the thumping of the blades. The pilot spotted an area about fifty yards to the north of them where he might possibly set his machine down. Since this difficult rescue was taking place on the steepest side of the mountain, he had no choice but to risk his life and the lives of the crew by setting the chopper down with only one wheel barely touching the ground. The rotor continued to spin with minimal clearance between the tip of the blade and the side of the mountain. The scary part for the pilot was when the wind would hit the tail rotor and push the tail section closer to the rocks. Because of the experience of the pilot and the rescue crew, the attempt was successful.

The climber did not survive his ordeal unscathed: he lost most of his toes to frostbite. A nurse said his back was one solid bruise when he was admitted to the hospital.

Months after the rescue, he sent the rescue crew members a Christmas card thanking them for their outstanding performance with the difficult rescue that had saved his life. They later informed him that the rescue attempt would have been impossible in another 30 minutes because of the thickening and lowering of the cloud cover and the resulting deteriorating conditions.

After his ordeal this climber had some meaningful advice for others: "Climbing Mt. Shasta should be attempted only after serious examination. You do not want to be the subject of a mountain rescue search. Keep in mind that if you put yourself in a position of being rescued, you are also putting other people's lives on the line."

If you are climbing the mountain for the first time, then make sure you do it with another climber, preferably someone who has experience. Solo climbing should only be done by the experienced mountaineer and not a first-time climber.

CLIMBING GEAR

"Quality mountain gear is expensive but don't let the cost deter you, make your first climb with borrowed or rented gear."

Having good quality and well fitting gear is extremely important when climbing a mountain such as Shasta because it can make the difference between an enjoyable experience and a dangerous one. Poor fitting boots, a pack that is too small, or the wrong type of stove can all make or break your experience when climbing the mountain. Worse, things such as an inadequate sleeping bag, a tent that is not up to the task of wind and snow, or improper clothing can quickly become life threatening at high altitude.

Of equal importance you need to understand how to use the equipment BEFORE you set out to climb the peak. Setting up the tent in your backyard and making a practice base camp is the best way to assure yourself that all of your gear functions correctly.

If you are a first time climber it does not mean that you need to make large equipment purchases. When possible you can rent or borrow the appropriate gear to ease the initial costs. Then, when you have gained experience you will have a better idea of what type of equipment works best for you.

Visit our Mountain Tips and Mountain Tricks: Short YouTube™ videos on gear & packing tips: www.swsmtmt.com

PACK CHECKLIST

Pack checklists are an important part of planning your trip on any mountain. High up on Mt. Shasta you do not want to forget an essential items such as a lighter for the stove or your sunglasses. A SWS Mountain Guides Mt. Shasta equipment list is located in Appendix C.

BACKPACKS

Today's mountaineers rely almost exclusively upon the

internal frame backpack for getting around in the mountains. These packs carry the weight closer to the center of gravity and tend to be more stable than the older external frame packs. For a multiday climb on Shasta a pack volume between 65 (3500 cubic inches) and 85 (5000 cubic inches) liters is ideal. A popular backpack amongst our guides is the Black Diamond Mission 75 liter because it is right in this size range and is a very simple and well fitting pack. Whether you are borrowing or purchasing a backpack for your climb it is

Black Diamond™ internal frame backpack

important to think of a backpack much like a pair of boots, i.e.… fit is everything. The hip belt should sit squarely and snugly on the iliac crest of your hips without maxing out the buckle straps and then all other straps are adjusted around this point. The underarm straps should be pulled at least four-fingers below the armpit. The load-lifter strap, behind the head, ideally comes up at a 45° angle thus pulling the weight up off the shoulders while simultaneously pulling the pack closer to the center of gravity. When fit properly the pack should feel like 75-85% of the weight is on the hips and lower back with the remainder on the shoulders. If the pack is not fitted properly it can feel cumbersome and be extremely painful to carry. This can cause an already physically demanding venture to become quite unpleasant and perhaps precluding you from even making it to base camp let alone the Summit. Do not go cheap here! One last note for the ladies out there, look for women's specific packs. If it fits you well you will not regret it.

TENTS

The style of a tent you choose depends on what time of year you climb, the weather, and how many people will be sleeping in it. A good tent can literally be a lifesaver if the weather takes a turn for the worst. We have found over many years of guiding on Mt. Shasta that it is best to always use a four season tent even during the summer months. Even so, we still lose 3-4 tents to high winds every year particularly during the months of May and June. Having said

Black Diamond™ four-season tent

that, there have been times when we have slept outside in our sleeping bags and were just fine, but it is always best to play it safe and bring a good tent. A free-standing tent is preferred because of ease of set up and stability.

Tents are rated by the season, for instance a three-season tent is rated for 3 seasons excluding winter while a four-season tent has a winter rating and is capable of withstanding higher winds and snowstorms. Mountaineering tents are expensive but the quality is superb, as most tents offer waterproofing, wind-proofing, and breathable materials which make the tents more suitable for backpacking or mountaineering. You will have to think of the weight involved when you are considering which tent to use as well as how many people will be sharing the tent. Two to five pounds is about the weight you will want to carry per a person.

To save on weight we recommend not bringing a ground cloth for your tent, especially if your base camp will be on snow. It is not necessary and we never use them even if we are camping on dirt or rocks! When setting up your tent it is imperative that you attach the rain fly securely and that you guy out the tent in at least four directions, especially if it is windy or you expect wind.

Here are some things to consider when choosing a tent:
1. Size, weight, and design.
2. Waterproof and wind-proof.
3. Structural strength.
4. Can you cook inside?
5. Color, a bright color tent is easy to spot when returning back to camp.
6. Freestanding or not freestanding.
7. Mosquito netting.
8. Plenty of room for yourself and your gear.

9. Plenty of space for your tent mate.
10. Ventilation holes and windows.

Another option available to eliminate the weight of a tent is to sleep in a bivouac sack. A "bivy" sack is designed for lightweight travel and provides protection from the wind and snow. The bottom of the "bivy" sack is made with coated nylon and goes against an insulated ground pad. The "bivy" sack is intended for one person only. Please keep in mind that your gear will have to remain outside in the elements if you are to use a "bivy" sac and all cooking will have to be done outside as well.

This brings up the topic of cooking inside your tent. Every year there are reports of climbers or backpackers dying in their tents from carbon monoxide poisoning while cooking in their tents. You **MUST** have adequate ventilation for cooking, or better yet do not cook inside your tent, but if you must, cook in a well ventilated vestibule instead.

SLEEPING BAG AND PAD

The sleeping bag is one of the more important items of the trip. If your tent blew down the hill and the chipmunks ate your food, you would still stay warm if you had a good quality sleeping bag. Your bag should be lightweight, warm, and easily compressible. A form-fitting hood and a zipper that works also add to the comfort. Some bags provide an insulated collar for extra warmth around the shoulders.

Sleeping bags are categorized by their temperature ratings in ideal conditions. These temperature ratings range from +50°F to -40°F. We recommend a rating of 20°F to 10°F for summer mountaineering and a 0°F to -20°F rated bag for winter mountaineering on Mt. Shasta.

We highly recommend sleeping bags stuffed with down. Down bags are lighter and compress to a smaller size than synthetic bags plus down bags will not lose their insulation rating over time like synthetic bags. There is one major disadvantage in using down over synthetic and that is down loses most of its loft when it gets wet. This, however, is not a major factor when climbing Mt. Shasta since your first time climbing should be done in the summer. As a matter of fact, we have rarely ever had a problem using down bags over the course of guiding trips for several decades and on several continents! Your bag will also be well protected in a stuff bag (we recommend a compression sack for down bags, but never use one on a synthetic bag) and in inclement weather a trash bag can be used for extra protection. A synthetic bag will dry quickly if it gets wet, but it also weighs more than the down bag. Both styles of sleeping bags work well on Mt. Shasta.

A good sleeping pad is also an essential item if you plan on getting any sleep at all at base camp. You will most likely find yourself camping on snow on most routes on this peak so a sleeping pad needs to be thick enough to insulate you from the snow. We recommend either a closed cell foam pad at least half an inch in thickness or a Thermarest type pad that is rated for winter camping. While a full length pad is nice you really only need a three quarter length pad and then put your empty backpack under your feet when sleeping.

ICE AXE

The ice axe is the quintessential tool of the mountaineer. It is essential on almost any serious snow or ice climb that you could ever endeavor. Today's modern ice axe comes in scores of sizes, styles, and designs each with their own specific purpose and place in mountaineering. Traditional axes work for general mountaineering, whereas ice tools may be preferable for vertical ice. Some ice axes are even incorporated into ski poles, such as the Black Diamond Whippet, allowing ski mountaineers to self arrest when skiing on icy terrain. For the purposes of climbing most routes on Mt. Shasta, the ice axe of choice is the traditional mountaineering axe such as the Black Diamond Raven. These can range in length from 55cm upwards of 85cm. The appropriate length can be found by standing upright with the axe in your hand and letting the axe hang free. The spike of the axe should be just above your ankle.

The parts of the mountaineering ice axe include the head for gripping the axe, the pick for self-arrest, the adze for chopping ice and snow, and the spike for driving into the snow for an anchoring point. In order to properly know how to use your axe it is imperative that you take a lesson with a professional instructor. Make sure to become proficient with ice axe and self-arrest skills as these can save your life!

*Black Diamond™
adjustable
trekking poles*

SKI POLES

Collapsible ski poles or trekking poles are a must when climbing, especially when traveling with a heavy pack on slippery volcanic talus. Ski poles should be used to get you to base camp, and may even be helpful when climbing to the Summit. The poles provide excellent balance and stabilization, and they also allow you to keep some of the weight off your lower body. Any style of poles will work for you as long as they are adjusted properly. For uphill travel, poles are adjusted properly when the elbows are at a 90° angle. Lengthening the poles for downhill travel will help take stress off the knees and legs. Telescopic poles are convenient because you can collapse them and carry them securely in your pack when they are not in use. Ski poles are a benefit to the climber but must never be substituted for an ice axe.

CRAMPONS

Crampons come in many different styles and designs. Most crampons, like the ice axe, are made from aluminum or chrome-molybdenum steel. Some designs have different styles of straps, points, and hinges. Backpackers might use 4- or 6- point crampons to cross an occasional snowfield. While the Modern 10-point crampons are adequate for climbing Avalanche Gulch. We still prefer the 12-point models offering more secure footing with the additional two points that are added. Crampons made for climbing on snow and glaciers are referred to as "hinged" or "semi-rigid" recognized by the adjustable bar in the middle of the crampon. Steer

Black Diamond™ 12 point Sabretooth Crampon

away from rigid crampons or "technical crampons," these are better suited for the ice climber who wants to tackle the more technical routes on Mt. Shasta.

The two most basic styles of crampons are the step-in and strap-on crampons in addition to a hybrid system which combines the two. Step-in crampons are specific to one style of boot requiring the boot to have both a stiff sole and a lip for the crampons to attach (example: double plastic boots). Therefore, you cannot use step-ins with all types of boots. Strap-ons and hybrid systems on the other hand, can be used with any boot provided it has a stiff enough sole.

Always bring your boots along when renting to purchasing crampons to make sure the system works with your type of footwear. For the purposes of general mountaineering either product will work equally as well. Note: There is a right and left crampon; look for the little foot stamped on the adjustment bar or on the crampon itself.

HELMETS

While you might see many climbers climbing without a helmet we highly recommend wearing one above Helen Lake or on any route on the mountain when you are above 10,000 feet. We have just seen way too many near misses as well as hits on Mt. Shasta over the years. While almost any helmet would be better than nothing, helmets made specifically for climbing are the way to go. The Half Dome helmet made by Black Diamond is a good example of a lightweight mountaineering helmet.

SNOW SHOVEL

Mountaineering snow shovels are generally made of aluminum with a telescopic handle. A snow shovel is crucial during an early season climb and may be useful during a late summer climb. You need a snow shovel for digging snow shelters, leveling off tent sites, and carrying clean snow to your camp for melting water. Snow shovels are also a necessary piece of equipment for digging snow pits for determining avalanche conditions as well as digging out anyone who might get caught in an early season avalanche. These lightweight shovels break down for easy packing and offer very little weight due to their aluminum composition.

CLOTHING

Good quality clothing protects your body from the cold and fierce winds that can generated on Mt. Shasta. Wearing lightweight breathable clothing also protects your skin from the blazing sun when it gets too hot. Clothing should be worn in multiple layers, allowing you to remove or add layers when temperature changes occur. The layers are as follows: a layer next to the skin, an interior insulating layer, and an exterior protective layer.

LAYER NEXT TO THE SKIN

The layer next to the skin consists of socks and long underwear. Socks insulate your feet as well as provide a cushion and perspiration absorbent. Cotton socks should be avoided since they absorb water which ruins their insulating qualities. You should look for good quality socks made from either synthetic or merino wool. We are partial to socks made by Point6.

Many climbers wear a polypropylene liner sock under their wool or synthetic outer sock. The liner sock wicks away the moisture from the foot to the outer sock. Make sure to ask about this when purchasing your socks. Sock designer Point6 actually recommends not wearing a liner because their mountaineering sock actually wicks better than the polypropylene, but the choice is really yours. For the outer sock there is a design specifically made for mountain climbing which has extra padding under the heel and metatarsal bones. The padding absorbs impact and reduces friction that causes blisters and calluses. Medium density padding at the shin, ankles, and toes provides cushioning from boot folds and lace pressure. The arch has spandex for support and a wool toe for warmth. A fully padded sock of this type is worth purchasing even if you use it only for one climb.

Long underwear provides ventilation and warmth to the body and should also be made of polypropylene, capiline, or a merino wool material. This type of material is lightweight, flexible, and has the ability to wick moisture away from your skin much like the socks. When breathable material gets wet, it will dry much faster than cotton. There is an old saying in mountaineering —"cotton kills!"

INTERIOR INSULATING LAYERS
The insulating layers usually consist of wearing some type of fleece/wool jacket or even a down jacket and fleece/wool pants. The ideal method is to wear one of the several styles of breathable shirts available that wicks away moisture from the skin as you perspire. A fleece insulating layer makes for a great piece whether it is a traditional fleece or a soft shell piece. These are great pieces of clothing because they provide a good deal of warmth and wind resistance, they are durable, and they continue to insulate well even when wet. The soft shell pieces are fleece material with a smooth outer finish that allows better wind and water resistances. In good weather these are often used as both an insulating layer and the shell layer.

Finally, down jackets provide the most insulation for the

Our guide Brady well layered with his Millet Puffy!

weight. When the weather is colder this is often a good piece to have. Modern down jackets come pre-coated with Pertex© or some other water resistant material so that the down does not get damp easily. In very wet conditions; however, it is best to use these in conjunction with an exterior shell layer of some sort. You would be hard pressed to find any mountaineering guide who goes out in the mountains without his or her down jacket.

EXTERIOR PROTECTIVE LAYER
The exterior protective layer, or shell, provides protection from the wind, rain, snow, and/or sun. Today, technology has far more types of materials and fabrics than can be reasonably discussed here. What is important is that whatever type of shell you choose that it be windproof, waterproof, and breathable. This layer should provide some degree of warmth but mostly it is designed to keep the elements off of your insulating layers.

GAITERS

Gaiters are another piece of outer wear that is important to have because they really help to keep snow out of your boots, especially when you are glissading. Make sure you get a large enough pair to fit over your big mountaineering boots.

HATS

According to the Wilderness Medicine Newsletters up to 55% of body heat can be lost through your head during physical activity. In cold or severe environments, such as Mt. Shasta, a wool or polyester hat can make a big difference in keeping your entire body warm. You might also consider a facemask to protect your nose and mouth. A popular piece among climbers is the balaclava which is multipurpose since it covers the face and neck as well as the head. When conditions permit you can use the balaclava as a neck warmer or just for the top of the head. During sunny, windless days, some climbers wear a desert-style hat which covers the back of the head, neck, and the sides of the face and helps prevent them from getting sunburned. We cannot stress enough the importance of protecting your skin from both sun and cold and having the proper headwear goes a long way in accomplishing this.

GLOVES

Much like your other clothing, the layers and styles of your gloves will be dictated by the weather conditions on the mountain. In warmer conditions a good pair of waterproof insulated gloves may be all that you need. When conditions are colder and/or when winds are higher you might think of adding synthetic or merino wool liners much like the liners for your socks. Mittens or overmitts may also be worn, though they do decrease dexterity. They are, however, the warmest choice for protecting your fingers from frostbite. This can make handling your ice-axe or other tools cumbersome but in extreme conditions it may be the only thing that keeps your hands warm. Many guides take several different pairs of gloves/mittens so they can change them in accordance with changing conditions.

BOOTS

There is an endless supply of hiking boots on the market today and a wide range of leather, plastic, and hybrid (combining plastic and leather components) mountaineering boots. If you are an experienced climber, you will already know what style of boots you will need. For the first-time climber, you might plan on renting a pair of double, plastic mountaineering boots from one of the local gear shops. If you are climbing the Avalanche Gulch route mid to late summer, a durable leather or synthetic boot can be sufficient or light mountaineering boots are also available for rent.

The "doubles" are a two-boot system with an insulating liner that keeps your feet warm and dry inside of the hard plastic, waterproof shell. Some manufactures make mountaineering boots that are specifically designed for women's feet. When trying boots on, it is important that your heels fit firmly in place while allowing your toes to move freely in the toe box. Having toe room will give your feet the clearance they need when hiking downhill as well as not impeding circulation that can contribute to frostbite.

Climbing Mt. Shasta can be very rewarding, so don't spoil it by choosing the wrong style boot or boots that do not fit properly. We cannot stress this enough. **Take your time** when trying on boots to ensure yourself a proper fit.

COOKWARE

There are two different types of mountaineering stoves; ones which use liquid fuel and others which use compressed gas in a canister for fuel. Either type of stove will work well for you on Mt. Shasta. Make sure your stove works before you leave home, and always take extra fuel for melting snow for drinking and cooking.

We at SWS Mountain Guides allocate about 5-6oz of white gas per person per day and this is generally enough for cooking and melting snow. Oh, and please do not forget the matches and lighter. We have learned the hard way that it is very difficult to light a stove without some kind of incendiary device!

As for the rest of your cookware, you only really need a pot with a lid that is big enough for the party you are climbing with and maybe a pot gripper and a stirring spoon. The pot gripper is really nice to have so that you do not have to worry about burning yourself on the pot. If you are melting snow it is a good idea to take a pot larger than you think you might need because it takes a very large volume of snow to produce any significant amount of water.

FOOD

Although a lack of appetite is a common side effect of high altitude it does not change the fact that your body is in constant need of calories. Some estimates say climbing a peak can take upwards of 6,000 to 9,000 calories per day. No matter how much snacking you do, your body will still crave foods that have high energy content. Mountaineering cuisine can be satisfying and useful only if the food provides the necessary fuel to keep you going. Carbohydrates, protein, and fats provide the body with the energy needed, but only in the right proportions. A dietician, sports trainer, or experienced climber can offer some worthwhile advice on what your body may need for energy on the climb. For some of our guides favorite recipes visit SWS Mountain Guides at www.swsmtns.com/recipes.html

Taking meals that only need to be boiled will eliminate the need to carry excess pots. This also reduces the quantity of dirty dishes to be cleaned. If you strategically plan your meals, you should be able to use a small pot, one cup, a bowl, and a spoon. Meals that are quick and easy to prepare include instant soups, noodles, rice, hot drinks, oatmeal, and juice. You should also consider taking along granola bars, energy bars, crackers, trail mix, dehydrated fruits, bread, or pretzels. Cheese offers one of the highest caloric foods per weight and often does not need to be refrigerated, but some folks have trouble digesting fatty foods at altitude. If snow is available for refrigeration, you can eat in style by taking along cream cheese and cold cuts for your bagels. There have been countless times where folks have offered us money for the fantastic sandwiches that some of us build up on the Summit with cream cheese, avocado, ham, and tomato!

SUNGLASSES

A high quality pair of sunglasses and good sunscreen are the keys to surviving the direct ultraviolet rays up on Mt. Shasta. At an elevation of 10,000 feet, the ultraviolet rays are 45-50 percent greater than at sea level. The radiance of the sun combined with the thinning of the atmosphere and the rays reflecting off the snow are strong enough to burn the retinas in your eyes, causing a painful condition known as snow blindness. Snow blindness is temporary, but it could prevent you from reaching the Summit. Your sunglasses must filter 100% of the ultraviolet light and the frames should be equipped with side shields.

There are so many different styles of sunglasses that you may be wondering what is the best pair for mountaineering? You should avoid using cheap sunglasses and stick to the two basic types of glasses which are made of either a polycarbonate or optical glass lens.

The glacier-style sunglasses are the best type of sunglass to use during the summer months. Glacier glasses generally offer a polarizing filter that is sandwiched between layers of optical glass to cut through the glare. Some glacier glasses offer a double gradient optical glass which allows the lenses to change from medium to dark amber. Glacier-style sunglasses are also noted for their wrap-around temples. The wrap-around temples help keep the glasses on your head, thereby eliminating frame straps. The nylon frames are made for comfort and the side shield for protection. Without having side protection the corner of the eyes can get burned.

If you plan on skiing down from the Summit or are expecting high winds it may be advisable to also bring a pair of goggles. Please note that whatever you decide upon for your glasses, buy the best you can afford and USE them! You would not believe the number of climbers we see climbing without eye protection. They are courting disaster.

SUNBLOCK

The body's skin is capable of being burning severely at high elevations. A long-sleeved shirt is recommended, but it is sometimes not practical on a hot summer day. Many climbers wear shorts, but they often forget to put sunscreen on their legs which often results in severe burns, especially right behind

Applying Sunscreen 4-5 times a day is common on Mt. Shasta.

the knees. OUCH! Sunscreen needs to be applied any time you are in the mountains, even on cloudy or cold days. A sunscreen with a sun protection factor (SPF) of 30 or higher is a necessity. A cream that is waterproof and sweat-proof is optimal for mountaineering. Good quality sun blocks can be purchased almost anywhere, and are well worth the investment. Lip protection is super important, as well. The lips should be coated frequently with zinc oxide or lip balms with a sun block protection of at least 15 SPF. On a typical Mt. Shasta summit day many of us will apply sunscreen and lip balm at least four or five times, so keep slathering it on!

BATTERIES

Most of the software items on the pack list are self-explanatory; however, you need to remember that cold temperatures at high altitudes can cause camera batteries to lose power rapidly and die on you. Missing a shot from the Summit because of a weak battery can be quite frustrating. Always use new batteries in your camera, flashlight, and head lamp and bring an extra pair. When it is cold keeping your batteries inside your jacket pocket will help them last longer.

TRAVELING ON SNOW

SNOWSHOES

For many mountaineers the snowshoe is the preferred method of travel when the snow is soft. They are simple, inexpensive, and do not require any additional skills to use. Snowshoes are easily attached to your mountaineering boots much like a strap-on crampon and provide a great deal of mobility. There is not a great difference in styles or design but it is important to find a snowshoe that has sufficient surface area to support the weight of both you and your backpack. It is worthwhile to note here that for a climbing snowshoe it is really recommended that they have a heel riser built into the snowshoe. The snowshoe preferred by us here at SWS Mountain Guides is one of the MSR models such as the Ascent or Explore. To find out current conditions and whether or not you may need snowshoes you can always contact the local guide companies or gear shops.

SKIS

Backcountry and ski mountaineering skis are designed specifically to be lighter weight than their in-bounds brethren so as to move as efficiently as possible. Much like regular skis they have a wide variety of flex patterns and side cuts for all conditions. Finding the right backcountry ski is mostly a matter of finding the styles and features that fit the skier's style and the conditions they will be used in.

BINDINGS

Despite dozens of designs and manufacturers, all backcountry ski bindings have the one common thread of a "free" heel. By having the heel of the boot unattached and a hinge at the toe of the ski boot the skier can walk uphill with the ski simply sliding along under the foot.

For the telemark skier the boot is never locked down as the boot and the binding work as a hinge. In the case of some of the newer binding by such as the Black Diamond O1s, the binding may even have an extra hinge for a touring mode that gives the skier a greater range of motion to allow for greater glide length and more efficient travel. When traveling downhill the telemarker uses different downhill techniques to turn the ski, and until recent improvements in binding technology, this was the preferred method of backcountry skiing.

In the case of alpine touring (AT) or Randonee bindings the skier can lock the heel down once he has achieved their uphill objective. In this manner the binding is similar to a telemark binding when used for uphill travel, but then acts like a traditional alpine ski during the downhill mode. These bindings have become the most popular ski binding amongst backcountry skiers and ski mountaineers in recent years.

SPLITBOARDS

Splitboards are the newest addition to the backcountry world and already have over a dozen designers and are gaining popularity rapidly. These snowboards are cut down their long axis and allow the board to be separated (split) into two individual skis for uphill travel. The bindings are hinged similarly to backcountry ski binding allowing the rider to move uphill. These skis are then reattached and the bindings are placed back into their downhill position for downhill travel like a regular snowboard.

SKINS

Used by skiers, and now splitboarders, skins are the key piece of equipment that has enabled uphill travel on skis for hundreds of years. The use of skins has dated back for almost 4,000 years and they were used throughout the arctic regions, North America, Europe and even Mongolia. Strips of animal hides, usually seal fur, were attached to the underside of wooden skis. Smooth in one direction and course in the other, these skins allowed snow travelers to move uphill over the snow.

Despite new technology the concept of skins has essentially remained the same since ancient days. Today animal pelts have given way to synthetic fibers with adhesive backings. Thousands of fibers lay flat and remain smooth when traveling in the uphill direction, but then engage the snow to prevent the ski from sliding back down the hill when they are weighted. With so many fibers working in unison, today's ski mountaineers can ascend steep angles at relatively quick speeds.

A LAST NOTE ON COST

The total cost of all this gear can be astounding if it were to be purchased all at once. You do not have to spend a ton of money to get started in mountaineering. It is possible to rent or borrow much of the gear when first starting out. If you do borrow a backpack or boots make sure that they fit properly. After your first climb you will also have a better idea of the right type of gear that will suit your needs. Buying some of the software items on the pack checklist is fine, as long as you wait before purchasing the hardware. Also make sure you know the history of the gear that you rent or borrow. You do not want to use a rope that your buddy has been using to tow his car! Appendix B has a list of mountaineering stores and websites that specialize in quality backpacking, mountaineering, and outdoor gear.

PREPARATION

THREE WEEKS BEFORE

"It was our preparation, knowledge, and experience that kept us alive."
Rachel Kelsely - British Mountain Climbing Instructor

Preparing to climb Mt. Shasta can be very chaotic since you will be taking care of unfinished business, feeding your pets, and doing some last-minute grocery shopping before the trip. You will probably also be working at your job and at the same time trying to pack and assemble your gear. The next thing you will be doing is trying to convince your family members that you plan on coming back alive. It is always good practice to let your family members or friends know what route you are climbing and when you plan to come down off the mountain. Explain to them that you have read this book and have taken all the precautions mentioned. You are mentally and physically prepared and feel fully qualified to make a successful ascent to Mt. Shasta's Summit.

One of the most important things to do before you leave home is to check the climbing, avalanche, and weather reports. If possible, you need to try to schedule your climb around Mt. Shasta's weather and not according to your personal schedule. Conditions can change rapidly in the mountains, especially in the winter months. Before climbing, make sure there are no storms forecasted and do not rely on long-range weather forecasts because they are usually only accurate for a few days. You should inquire daily from all sources about weather conditions.

Most first-time climbers usually have to buy, borrow, or rent the proper climbing gear. You should consult someone who has climbed Mt. Shasta or someone with experience in climbing or backpacking. If you already have good quality backpacking equipment, you will probably only need to rent a pair of double mountaineering boots, an ice axe, and crampons. You should reserve your rental equipment at least two weeks in advance or more for the peak month of June. (For local Mt. Shasta Rental Shops See Appendix A).

PACKING YOUR PACK

Packing your pack for the first time will be time consuming and will no doubt be the most frustrating part of your trip.

Anyone who has gone camping before realizes how important it is to pack with proper care. Packing to climb Mt. Shasta will take some extra thought since

Re-adjusting your pack weight on the trail is OK!

each item has to be advantageously placed. You should start accumulating your gear, clothing, and equipment at least one month before the climb. When you get ready to pack, you may find it simpler to lay all your gear on the floor and pack everything at once. Doing this will eliminate the "what did I forget" syndrome and also give you plenty of time for better organization.

Weight distribution is the most important rule for a climber's pack. When your pack is loaded, is should not weight more than one third of your weight. Carrying an overweight pack or a sloppy pack can cause many problems, resulting in wasted energy and increasing the possibility of falling. Overweight packs are hard on the body and will tend to make you very cranky and tired, especially if you are experiencing some grueling pain on your shoulders and back. Make your pack as light as possible because you will find the pack seems to get heavier the longer it is on your back.

Water will be the heaviest item in your pack (weighing in at 2.2 lbs per liter) and it is by far the most important thing you carry. You should pack the water using wide mouth liter containers (capacity of 3-4 liters) such as Nalgene bottles and plan on carrying at least 2-3 liters of water with you. If you are climbing one of the routes out of the Bunny Flat trailhead you can initially pack in 1 liter of water and then fill up all four liters containers at the Sierra Club Foundation's Cabin at Horse Camp. You will, however, need to check with the Ranger Station or the Sierra Club Foundation before climbing to find out if the Cabin's spring is running and free of snow, otherwise you will need to leave the trailhead with all bottles full.

Any pack you choose should allow you to carry the weight close to your body with the heavy items loaded near the bottom of the mid third of your backpack, but for sure above your sleeping bag. By loading the pack this way, your legs and back take the weight instead of your shoulders and the heavier items are closer to your center of gravity thus decreasing the amount of sway. Using an internal-frame pack, you have the option of strapping your tent to the, sides, bottom or placing it inside at the very top. When you arrive at base camp, the first thing you will need is your tent so if it is not easily accessible, you will be forced to unload the contents of your pack out on the ground or the snow which can be bad if the wind is blowing.

Your lunch, sunscreen, and water have to be accessible while you are climbing, so keep those important items handy. You should also keep your crampons accessible by strapping them to the outside of your pack along with your ice axe and sleeping pad. Packing is like a chess game; each move has to be carefully planned out in advance. If you have to pack several times, it will be worth the extra effort to get it the way you want it. Do not expect to pack a perfect pack the first time, as it usually takes several climbing trips to get the hang of it. While climbing to base camp, you are more likely to need some extra clothing or food rather than your cookware, so pack them on top.

It is a good idea to weigh your pack once it is loaded. You can do this using your bathroom scale by weighing yourself with the pack on and then with it off. Doing this will give you an idea on exactly just how much weight you can handle. If your pack weighs in at 60 pounds and you make your climb and find out the weight is too much to handle, you will know next time just how much weight will need to be reduced. To test for balance and stability, walk around your yard at home with a full pack. The more time you spend at home organizing and testing your pack, the fewer the chances you will need to tear it apart on the trail.

You will probably finish packing at the last minute on the night before your climb, and the likely you will not to bed until late. Being nervous and excited about climbing a mountain is normal, especially if it is your first time. Every climber has the jitters the night before, including well-seasoned mountaineers. You will probably be so apprehensive the day before that it may prevent you from getting a good night's rest. Do not let this worry you because climbing to base camp can be done with only a few hours of sleep.

The following morning you will find your adrenaline takes over because of the eagerness and excitement you have anticipating reaching the top of Mt. Shasta. Make sure you arrive at Bunny Flat trailhead at a reasonable time in the morning. The earlier you get started climbing to base camp the more time you will have to select a choice camp site, to rest, and to get accustomed to the high altitude. In addition, an early start will help insure you are traveling on still-frozen snow and the cooler temperatures will help you avoid trekking through slushy snow and becoming overheated.

AVALANCHE GULCH
"AN ASCENT"

STARTING POINT

The trailhead to the Avalanche Gulch, Casaval Ridge, and
the West Face routes begins at Bunny Flat, milepost 11, on
the Everitt Memorial Highway. To get there from Interstate
5, take the central exit to the city of Mt. Shasta, which will
put you on Lake Street. Continue east through the Mt.
Shasta Blvd. intersection, through the merge with
Washington Drive, and its resulting curve to the north. Go
through the stop sign at the next intersection. Across this
intersection is the beginning of the Everitt Memorial
Highway, or A10, as it is marked on some maps. Drive 11
miles, referring to the milepost markers on the highway,
winding up the mountain to the Bunny Flat parking lot at an
elevation of 6,860 feet.

GETTING THERE

The highway is county-maintained year round, including
snow-removal services during the winter months. The two-
lane, paved road is kept in excellent shape for any type of
vehicular travel, but during the winter months, road
conditions can change rapidly because of snowstorms and
rock fall. Sometimes, especially in heavy snowfall, the road
may not get plowed until the late afternoon. You should
always carry a shovel and tire chains in your vehicle in the
winter, and drive slowly when the road is icy. If you arrive at
the Bunny Flat parking lot before the road has been plowed,

Bunny Flat Trailhead parking area

park close to the snow bank, allowing the snowplow plenty of room to clear the parking lot.

In 1912 a wagon road was built from the town of Sisson (Mount Shasta) to Horse Camp. Many years later, in 1927, it was decided build a road for automobiles. The road, then called the Snowline Highway, was finally completed in 1940, not to Horse Camp, but to Panther Meadow. In 1934, the yet uncompleted highway was renamed the Everitt Memorial Highway. The change was proposed by the American Legion to honor the memory of John Samuel Everitt, then the supervisor of the Shasta National Forest, who died in the line of duty in the Bear Springs fire. The fire was on the slopes of Mt. Shasta, and the place he died was in an area in which the road was being constructed.

Years ago, when the road was first plowed to the parking lot, local skiers used to practice in the meadow there, which soon became known as Bunny Flat; hence, the name Bunny

Flat parking lot. This small, flat meadow is also the place where many of our Ice Ax and Crampon clinics are conducted. On the north side of the parking lot, you will find a wooden building which has restrooms maintained year round and a small shelter to escape bad weather. Next to the building is a self issue station with a permit box containing the necessary Wilderness Area permits and Summit passes with a drop box for the Summit fees.

SECTION ELEVATION GAIN TIME

Bunny Flat to Horse Camp	6,860 ft to 7,880 ft	1,020 ft	1-2 hrs
Horse Camp to Spring Hill	7,880 ft to 8,400 ft	520 ft	45 min
Spring Hill to 50/50 Flat	8,400 ft to 9,400 ft	1,000 ft	1-2 hrs
50/50 Flat to Helen Lake	9,400 ft to 10,443 ft	1,043 ft	1-3 hrs

LET'S HIT THE TRAIL

The first section of the climb starts at the trailhead along the north side of the parking-lot restrooms; the trail leads to Horse Camp and the Sierra Club Foundation's Cabin. The trail is comparable to a well-traveled backpacking trail and is suitable for hikers of all ages. This 1.7-mile trail offers a splendid hike through white firs, mountain hemlocks, Pacific Silver firs (locally known as silver tips), and towering Shasta Red firs.

Hiking north across the Bunny Flat meadow, you will cross over a small ridge, the lower section of Green Butte Ridge. From this point you will have an easy hike for almost 30 minutes until the trail merges with the Sand Flat trail and makes an abrupt right turn to the northeast. You will then have a steady uphill hike for the next 30 minutes as the trail follows the forested ridge along the northwest side of Avalanche Gulch.

Looking off to your right into the wide-open Gulch gives you an idea as to what damage a roaring avalanche can do. Although avalanches are quite common in the upper reaches of the Gulch, in years of heavy snowfall an avalanche can even slide down to the lower end. The absence of trees at this destructive site proves that Avalanche Gulch is well named.

During the winter and the late spring when the trail is buried under snow, many climbers opt to take a shortcut right after crossing the lower end of Green Butte ridge and hike straight up the Gulch to reach or even bypass the Cabin. In the late spring when the snow melts from the lower end of the Gulch, it is not uncommon to find large pieces of debris from Red Banks that have tumbled down from past avalanches.

HORSE CAMP

In the early days before the road was built, climbers used to pack in with horses. The spot at timberline where they left their horses before setting out on foot was given the name "Horse Camp." When you finally reach Horse Camp, you can take off your pack, rest, and enjoy the spectacular view above timberline. When you look up at Avalanche Gulch, your eyes will be

Trail to Horse Camp

drawn to one of the most spectacular ridges on Mt. Shasta known as Casaval Ridge which is on the left or west side of Avalanche Gulch. To the far right of the Gulch, you will see a rolling, sloped ridge called Green Butte Ridge, which leads up and connects to the prominent, vertical Sargents Ridge. Sargents Ridge was named after John Sargent, a Forest Service Ranger, who spent a lot of time climbing Mt. Shasta. Avalanche Gulch Proper winds up the gully beneath Green Butte Ridge. This gully is named Avalanche Gulch Proper since it is the only gully in the Gulch that continues downwards without a moraine blocking its path.

Looking straight ahead, you will see a small hill known as Spring Hill. To the right of Spring Hill is the start of Climbers Gully which eventually leads up to the middle moraine nicknamed 50/50 Flat. Directly above the 50/50

Flat area is a steep hill which was named "Standstill Hill." Standstill Hill cannot be seen from the cabin although it is visible when you reach 50/50 Flat. At the top of the Standstill Hill is the moraine that climbers call Helen Lake. Straight up to the east from the moraine of Helen Lake, as viewed from the cabin, you can see The Heart, so named for its outward bulging, heart-like shape.

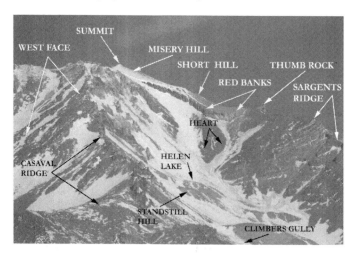

Landmarks looking up Avalanche Gulch.

The Red Banks rise immediately above The Heart with Thumb Rock (12,923 feet) sticking up to the east. The Red Banks is a very prominent formation that was ejected from Shasta's main Summit crater during a violent eruption that occurred about 10,000 years ago. Two successive flows of viscous magma, called a Tephra layer, covered the south shoulder of Sargents Ridge. When you view the Red Banks up close, it looks as though the red rock had flowed uncontrollably out from a concrete truck and was left there to harden without anyone applying the finishing touch.

Because of the snow, ice, and wind, the Red Banks are slowly eroding. Heavy snow accumulation and avalanches frequently send segments of the Red Banks plummeting down the Gulch.

THE CABIN

In 1922 the Sierra Club purchased 720 acres surrounding Horse Camp and began construction of the Sierra Club Lodge, later named the Shasta Alpine Lodge, sometimes called the Sierra Hut, but today usually referred to as "The Cabin." It is a large, one-room stone building with log poles supporting its metal roof, and a spring just outside the door to the south. The Cabin and private land in holding within the Wilderness Area is owned and managed by the Sierra Club Foundation.

James "Mac" Olberman, one of the Cabin's construction laborers, eventually became the first custodian or caretaker of the Cabin. Mac was custodian for 12 years and catered to the climbers by serving them meals and taking care of the grounds surrounding the Cabin. He spent time improving

The Cabin, at timberline, sits in a forest of Shasta Red Firs and Mountain Hemlocks with views of Avalanche Gulch behind.

the interior of the Cabin, but devoted most of his time building what is now known as the Olberman's causeway located behind the east side of the Cabin. With the help of others, Mac built this almost mile-long, rock causeway up to Spring Hill using a long digging bar which is still in the Cabin. After completing the causeway and making countless trips to the Summit, Mac's eyesight began to fail, forcing him to retire in the spring of 1937 at the age of 72. The beginning of the causeway marks the start of the traditional Avalanche Gulch Summit route.

During the summer months, the Sierra Club Foundation employs a full-time caretaker to watch over the Cabin and the surrounding grounds. The caretaker makes a home in a tent nearby and is available to answer any questions the climbers may have. On July 5, 1985, one such particular caretaker, Robert Webb, climbed (or should we say ran) from the Cabin to the Summit in a record-breaking time of 1 hour and 39 minutes. This is truly an accomplishment since it takes the average climber three to four hours just to reach Helen Lake. Once again on July 1998 Webb climbed to the Summit 6 times for a total of 37,572 feet in 23 hours and 22 minutes which at the time was believed to be a world record for the most elevation climbed on a mountain in a 24 hour period.

The Cabin, at timberline, sits in a forest of Shasta Red firs and Mountain Hemlocks with Avalanche Gulch beckoning beyond. The Cabin is never locked. However, camping is not allowed inside the Cabin except in an emergency, but you can go inside to escape the weather or look at some of the books in their library. There is also a guest book on the table which you may sign. Overnight camping sites are available around the Cabin for a small donation. During the winter, part-time caretakers and local volunteers watch over the Cabin, keeping the entrance clear of snow. Camp donation money is used for the upkeep of the Cabin and the solar, composting toilets which are the last such facilities on your way up the mountain.

If you have a friend or family member that has no desire to Summit Mt. Shasta, then Horse Camp makes for an ideal camping spot. During the early part of the summer, however, you will probably have swarms of mosquitoes for camping partners. Some climbers make the area around the Cabin their base camp so they can avoid carrying a full pack to Helen Lake. The drawback to this is that you have an extremely long, grueling climb to the Summit the following day. Unless you are extremely fit and acclimatized, or both, you should push on to Helen Lake to rest and acclimate to the altitude.

SHASTA'S PURE SPRING WATER

One of the highlights at Horse Camp is the spring located along the south side of the Cabin. The water is gravity fed from Spring Hill and piped to the surface at the Cabin, emptying into plastic feed barrels. There is no need for purification tablets or filters as Shasta's water is as pure as you will ever find. This is a good place to top off water before proceeding up Olberman's causeway. During the early climbing season, the spring can be buried under snow, so you must take enough water to get you to base camp. In the late spring, usually in the month of May, the Cabin's caretakers, the Wilderness Rangers, and a few volunteers will shovel the snow away from the spring.

Thirsty climbers at the Cabin quench their thirst with Shasta's pure, spring water.

Have you ever heard the saying, "Don't eat the yellow Snow?" Although this is good advice, the yellow snow will not hurt you, the pink snow growing in patches on the mountain must be avoided. The proper name for this pink-tinted snow algae is *Chlamydomonas nivalis*, but we call it watermelon snow due to its pink color and it actually does sort of smell like watermelon if you scoop some up and smell it. It has been suggested that consuming watermelon snow in large quantities can cause diarrhea. Quite often we get asked about the safety of the water and snow on the mountain. Most climbers believe that if the snow is clean that there is no reason to boil it before drinking it. If, however, you feel uncomfortable about the snow or any water source on Mt. Shasta then by all means boil or treat your water before consumption. It is, however, recommended to pre-filter your water though a bandana or towel to remove the fine silt which will clog your expensive water filter.

TRAIL TO HELEN LAKE –BASECAMP

Now that you have had a chance to grab a snack and fill your water bottles at Horse Camp it is time to put that beastly pack back on and head up towards Helen Lake. In the summer months, you follow the flat, rocky trail known as Olberman's causeway just east of the Cabin.

The route is the same during the early climbing season;

The beginning of the Olbermans's Causeway starts just beyond the Summit Trail marker.

however, the causeway will be buried under snow. The causeway ends at an elevation of 8,400 feet at Spring Hill. About 200 yards to the right of Spring Hill, Avalanche Gulch Proper curves up like a snake and eventually widens below Sargents Ridge. You do have the option of climbing the Gulch Proper to get to Helen Lake, but this path is longer and somewhat steeper. Most climbers generally stick to the Climbers Gully because it is a more direct route.

The Climbers Gully starts on top of Spring Hill and is a good place to rest, take off your pack, and get your first glimpse of the tremendous views to the south. Remember this is not a race to the top. Taking short rest stops every hour or so for a small sip of water and a small bite to eat will improve your chances of avoiding altitude sickness and of successfully arriving at base camp.

When you are half-way up the Gully you have two choices: continue up Climbers Gully or take the footpath up the large hill on your left that leads to the middle moraine or, as the locals call it, 50/50 Flat. In the old days 50/50 Flat was also known as Mac's Hogback. During the early climbing season, Climbers Gully is the definitely the best choice, but during the later part of the climbing season, either route is passable. The Gully has a steady, uphill grade and is not steep at any point. The large hill to the left is steep and composed of scree and talus; ski poles are helpful for stabilization. Either route will lead you to the same place, 50/50 Flat.

STANDSTILL HILL

When you reach 50/50 Flat, many stop to take a good rest before undertaking the final ascent up Standstill Hill to Helen Lake. A broad moraine, 50/50 Flat was carved out by advancing glaciers and makes an excellent and safe place to establish a base camp for those feeling too tired to push on to Helen Lake.

Standstill Hill was given its name by Steve Lewis during his climb to the Summit in June of 1995. The previous winter had produced unusually heavy snowfalls with more than 20 feet of snow in Avalanche Gulch. Steve was climbing on a weekend in the middle of the month just 1 week after a summer snowfall of 2 feet! The temperature had been very warm in the morning, and the bright sun glaring off the snow caused the snow to soften very rapidly. Steve and some other climbers found themselves post holing (sinking) up to their waists in snow while trying to climb this steep hill to Helen Lake. Fighting the heat and slushy snow, and carrying a full pack at this altitude, it was all they could do to take one step forward; it looked as though they were standing still, and so, Steve named the hill Standstill Hill.

Because of the increase in altitude and the preceding hours spent carrying a full pack on your back, you will find this hill difficult with snow or without. When the ground is covered in snow,

Long line of Climbers ascending "Standstill Hill"

most climbers ascend the left side of the hill. In the summer when the hill is free of snow, you may want to use the right-side approach which follows along the top of some moraines since the grade is not as steep. For stabilization on this hill, with or without snow coverage, ski poles are strongly recommended.

HELEN LAKE, I MADE IT

For those who choose to tackle Standstill Hill and ascend all the way to Helen Lake, you can call an end to your strenuous day's climb as Helen Lake is the last good camping spot with minimal threat of avalanche and rock fall. As for the Lake? Do not bother unpacking your fishing pole or bathing suit because you probably will not see a mountain lake. Helen Lake received its name in 1924 when mountaineer and botanist Edward Stuhl guided a climbing party to the Summit. One member of the party, Helen Wheeler, inquired about the name of the tiny, elegant lake, and Ed named it after her. That particular year must have been very dry because the tiny lake has only been seen in severe drought years when the snow at Helen Lake almost completely melts. Normally it is just a snowfield which lasts through the summer months into the following winter.

Looking to the southeast, you can see the snowcapped peak of Mt. Lassen in the distance. To the south, the town of McCloud and the Ski Park on Douglas Butte are also visible. On the southwest side of Green Butte Ridge, flower laden Panther Meadows can be seen at the base of Grey Butte. In the spring, if you hear the buzzing of what sounds like chainsaws, look down near the old Ski Bowl and you may see some snowmobilers doing some climbing of their own. Holidays and most summer weekends are usually crowded at Helen Lake. You can expect 20 tents or more set up on a normal summer weekend. On holiday weekends, Helen Lake has seen as many as 75 tents or more. It can seem worse than a campground at a popular resort. However, even if the camp area is crowded, you will always find a place to pitch a

tent. Arriving at Helen Lake in the late morning or the early afternoon will assure you of securing a good campsite.

Scattered Tents at Lake Helen.

Now it is time to set up your tent. It is very important that you do a good job at setting up and securing your tent because the winds can really howl up there. If you do not do a good job at guying out your tent, whether on snow or on the rocks, then even the slightest breeze can send your tent sailing down the hill like a kite and quite possibly account for a UFO sighting in town of Mt. Shasta. Practicing setting up your tent securely before your trip can eliminate any misfortunes.

Once your camp is set up, it is usually a good idea to prepare some hot soup to help stay hydrated and if time allows, maybe take a short nap. Do not forget about drinking some water; just remember the "3D's" words: drink, drink, and drink as much water as you can stand. Some of the new electrolyte replacement drinks work nicely as well and some actually taste good.

Cooking in the tent can be extremely hazardous so please cook outside or at the very least, if it is windy, cook in the vestibule, but make sure it is well ventilated. Although most mountaineering stoves are equipped with windshields around the burners to block the wind, they are inadequate. We will almost always cook outside even in the worst of weather. Building rock or snow walls around your stove can help block the wind. Whether you have a canister or a liquid fuel stove, you need to have a good stove stand for support. A small, aluminum, mess kit plate makes a good support as does a snow shovel blade.

Before nightfall you will need to have enough water to last you through breakfast the following morning and get you to the Summit. You need to have a minimum of 2 liters to get you to the Summit and back to base camp, but we highly recommend at least 3 if not 4 liters. It is nice to have another liter or so waiting for you at camp when you return so leaving a pot full of water at camp before you leave for the Summit is a good idea. Melting snow is time consuming, but it is a necessary chore to prepare for a Summit climb.

Now is also a good time to prepare your pack for Summit day. Your big pack cinched down will work just fine. The larger pack is much easier to pack, it carries easily, and its larger profile can actually serve to protect you from rock and icefall. It is worth noting here that we do NOT bother with carrying a separate Summit pack. Pack up your water bottles, lunch and snacks, sunglasses (super important and easy to forget in the dark), sunscreen, toilet paper, human waste pack out system just in case, sunhat, camera, and any other items you might want. You will most likely be wearing most of your layers in the morning so do not pack them.

You may find during your stay at Helen Lake that you need to use your human waste pack out system. Please help make everyone's experience on Mt. Shasta more enjoyable by walking away from the camp area when using the waste bags that are provided by the Forest Service.

GOODNIGHT

If you happen to get up in the middle of the night, try taking full advantage of the fantastic view awaiting you. Your midnight view will encompass the lights of the city of Mt. Shasta, Dunsmuir, and Redding to the south. Do not panic when you see the really bright lights to the southwest, it's not a UFO landing; it's only the Mt. Shasta Ski Park.

Between the lights, the moon, stars, and cold wind, night life on Mt. Shasta can be quite memorable. You may also notice that the scale of the mountain comes alive at night with the reflection of the moon and the bright light of the stars. Sometimes the moon shines so brightly you can read in your tent without the aid of a headlamp.

Early morning moon as it sets in the west.

LAKE HELEN TO THE SUMMIT PLATEAU

WAKE UP

Today is the big day Summit day. It has finally arrived. Everyone likes to sleep in when they are camping, but when daylight approaches, you should be out of the tent with your crampons on and ready to roll. If you melted snow the night before and your pack is loaded, all you need is a quick breakfast (bagel, instant oatmeal, tea, etc...) and you are on your way. We highly suggest getting up very early (called an Alpine Start) and start your climb most likely in the dark. Leaving Helen Lake by 4 am-5 am would be a great goal and this will give you plenty of time to reach the Summit and return to the parking lot in one day. For these early risers, you can use a headlamp strapped to your climber's helmet or, if fortunate, the light of a full moon.

If you start your climb on snow, you must use your crampons and ice axe and know how to use them. Helen Lake is also where we put our helmets on. If there is no snow, you have the option of using your ski poles or ice axe, but do not forget to pack you crampons for up higher. The ground is usually covered with snow until mid to late summer; after that the first snowfield may begin as far up as the area around The Heart, just below the Red Banks. During the late summer or early fall, this may be the only snowfield you will have to cross. This 2,500 foot, steep climb from Helen Lake to the Red Banks is the most strenuous section on the route. An average climber should expect to reach the Red Banks in 2-3 hours including short rest stops along the way.

Start your climb to the Red Banks by hiking straight up the middle of the Gulch. Keep trending more to the right until you reach the base of The Heart. The route gradually steepens and as the climb approaches the base of The Heart the route turns further to the right angling towards Thumb Rock. When you are making a steep ascent through this section, stay in good balance over your feet, plant your ice axe firmly with each step and keep

Climbers in-route from Helen Lake heading towards the Red Banks.

your crampons in full contact with the snow surface.

WATCH FOR ROCKS

Safety Alert! This is likely the most dangerous section of the Avalanche Gulch route. You need to be aware of rock fall

Watch for ice and rocks from the Red Banks

and chunks of ice that may come down from the Red Banks, the Trinity Chutes, and the other surrounding ridge tops. In the late spring and early summer, the morning sun strikes the Red Banks causing the ice that has formed to melt. Sometimes, if a chunk of ice breaks, it may contain rocks; when this happens, it normally plummets down the Gulch like fast-pitched baseballs, especially when the snow surface is frozen. Rocks and ice take the path of the least resistance, which is usually right down the center of the Gulch where you are climbing. When rocks fall on soft or slushy snow, they usually cannot roll very far because the snow acts like a baseball mitt, catching most of the rocks. Please do not take this to mean it is safer to climb late in the summer. Actually, late in the summer rock fall increases once most of the snow has melted. As professional guides we will actually halt all guiding activity in the Gulch once the snow has melted out up to The Heart or when rock fall becomes persistent. We feel that climbing on the snow is actually safer instead of the scree and talus.

We suggest keeping your rest breaks as brief as possible here and when stopped always have at least one member of your party keeping an eye out above for anything coming down. During the early summer months (May, June, and July) if there is rock and icefall coming off of Red Banks and the Trinity Chutes (the tall formations to the left of Red Banks), then we find it is generally safer to angle slightly higher up towards Sargents Ridge. The slope angle is steeper and physically more challenging, but this has the benefit of having less exposure to rock fall or ice fall from above. This is generally a safer decision but remember; **ALWAYS WEAR YOUR HELMET!**

Once you reach the base of The Heart, you will have two choices of which way to go. One choice is to climb to the left of The Heart towards Casaval Ridge. This route allows climbers to bypass the section of the mountain known as Short Hill and has the added benefit of being more or less absent of other climbers. This side of The Heart, however, is more dangerous because of the snow cornices that overhang on the far left side of the Red Banks and the rock fall from

The steep part of the climb, up to 38 degrees, heading to Thumb Rock.

both the Trinity Chutes and the Red Banks. Once on the left there is no good escape from these hazards. The chimneys (passageways) on this side of the Red Banks should only be climbed if you are an experienced climber who wants the challenge of climbing though these steep and narrow passageways.

Climbing to the right of The Heart towards Thumb Rock is the most popular and safest route to take, especially for novice climbers. This section steepens to 38° but it allows for a safer passage through the Red Banks. An important aspect to remember through this section is your footing. Concentrate on your footing and good ice axe technique, not on your fear. If you start to get frightened, you can easily lose your concentration which could result in a serious fall.

There are several options available for climbing through or around Red Banks from the right side of The Heart. The

first option is to approach the Red Banks directly from below and climb up through one of a series of chutes or chimneys. The

Climbing one of many chutes through the Red Banks.

largest chute, also called the main chute, on the Red Banks is located directly above The Heart and it usually holds snow year round. These chutes are steeper (up to 45°), can be icy, and lend themselves to higher risk of rock fall so climbing through them will require you to use your own judgment; the depth and hardness of the snow and steepness of the chute will be the deciding factors. They are, however, a much more direct path to Short Hill and the base of Misery Hill than the next option. Early in the summer, many climbers prefer to avoid the chutes by walking to the right toward the small saddle between the Red Banks and Thumb Rock and then traverse left over towards Short Hill. By midsummer when most of the snow has melted, the chutes are the preferred way to pass through the Red Banks. A word of warning if taking this option; when you top out next to Thumb Rock you are actually right on top of the Konwakiton Glacier and there is actually a pretty decent crevasse here so be careful and do not fall in!

CLIMBING ON SNOW AND ICE

While there are quite a few techniques available to climbers for ascending and descending snow and ice slopes safely,

explaining them in detail is beyond the scope of this book. If you have an interest in learning these skills in depth, it is best to take a clinic that teaches these respective skills. Your two basic choices when climbing up are either to traverse or go straight up. We have found that a steady traverse interspersed with brief periods of going straight up seems to work best for most folks. The boot technique we seem to employ the most is the modified French step technique or flat footing. This techniques can be used either while traversing or going straight up. Execution of this technique involves turning your body to the side so that it is diagonal to the slope and crossing your leg in front of the other to move up the fall line. If one leg gets tired, you can just turn your body around and ascend with the other leg leading the way.

If you want to rest your body, you will need to use the rest step or the locking leg rest. Keep your body sideways and diagonal to the slope and position your leg closest to the slope in front of you, allowing the leg muscles to relax. Support all of your body's weight on the leg downhill to the slope and thrust towards the back. Make sure that the foot supporting all your weight is firmly planted in the snow or ground and your leg is straight, allowing your body's weight to rest on the bones of your leg and not on the muscles. In our basic mountaineering courses we call this the "Rest Step."

While you are in the rest position, you may want to look back in the direction you came and enjoy the very spectacular phenomenon that occurs in the early morning hours on Mt. Shasta. When the sun rises behind the Red Banks, it casts a pyramid shadow of Mt. Shasta to the west. Depending upon the sun's angle, the shadow can cover Black Butte and most of the valley below. This breathtaking phenomenon can be seen while you are climbing to The Heart, so you may want your camera handy to capture this beautiful event.

Heading up Short Hill to the base of Misery Hill.

HOWLING WINDS

Once you have passed through the Red Banks, the weather conditions can change from virtually no wind at all to howling winds. The section from Thumb Rock to Misery Hill is well-known for severe winds, especially during the morning hours. Sometimes the winds are so intense that climbers have had to turn around to keep themselves from getting blown off the mountain. You may have heard previous climbers say they were "Blown off Misery Hill."

Cold temperatures that are accompanied with howling winds produce very severe wind chill factors. Climbing in this kind of weather without wearing the proper gear is inviting a case of frostbite. Generally during the summer, you can expect cold, windy conditions to exist in the morning hours, but by early afternoon the wind usually calms down and temperatures can become warm.

WIND CHILL CHART

Estimated Wind Speed in MPH	Actual Thermometer Readings (°Fahrenheit)											
	50	40	30	20	10	0	-10	-20	-30	-40	-50	-60
Calm	50	40	30	20	10	0	-10	-20	-30	-40	-50	-60
5	48	37	27	16	6	-5	-15	-26	-36	-47	-57	-68
10	40	28	16	4	-9	-21	-33	-46	-58	-70	-83	-95
15	36	22	9	-5	-18	-36	-45	-58	-72	-85	-99	-112
20	32	18	4	-10	-25	-39	-53	-67	-82	-96	-110	-124
25	30	16	0	-15	-29	-44	-59	-74	-88	-104	-118	-133
30	28	13	-2	-18	-33	-48	-63	-79	-94	-109	-125	-140
35	27	11	-4	-20	-35	-49	-67	-82	-98	-113	-129	-145
40	26	10	-6	-21	-37	-53	-69	-85	-100	-116	-132	-148

(Wind speeds greater than 40 mph have additional effect)

Little Danger

Danger! Exposed flesh can freeze.

Increasing Exposed flesh freezes in 1 minute

Great Danger! Exposed flesh freezes in 30 seconds.

Explanation: The wind-chill temperature is a measure of relative discomfort due to combined cold and wind. It was developed by Siple and Passel (1941) and is based on physiological studies of the rate of heat loss for various combinations of ambient temperature and wind speed. The wind-chill temperature equals the actual air temperature when the wind speed is 4 mph or less. At higher wind speeds the wind-chill temperature is lower than the air temperature and measures the increased cold stress and discomfort associated with wind. The effects of wind chill depend strongly on the amount of clothing and other protection worn as well as on age, health, and body characteristics. Wind-chill temperatures near or below 0 F indicate that there is a risk of frostbite or other injury to exposed flesh. The risk of hypothermia from being inadequately clothed also depends on the wind-chill temperature

BREAK TIME

Now that you have made it to the Red Banks, you can rest. Phew!! If you opted to traverse over to Thumb Rock, the saddle which sits below Thumb Rock provides a good resting spot to catch the warmth of the morning sun. Early in the summer, there is a snow-bridge (crossing) over the bergschrund of the Konwakiton Glacier which provides a passage over to the top of the Red Banks and thus Short Hill. Be extremely cautious if you cross over the snow bridge late in the afternoon; the softening of the snow may be just enough for you to fall into the glacier's deep crevasse. This is another reason why late-in-the-season climbers generally avoid going this way and go straight up the chutes instead.

LET'S GO TO MISERY HILL

After a fairly brief (5-10 minutes) rest period in the morning sunshine, you are now ready to finish the climb up Short Hill, at the top of the Red Banks, to the base of Misery Hill. Once you reach the top of Short Hill you will be at the base of Misery Hill (13,300 feet) which provides another excellent resting place. This is usually the place where we like to take a longer break, especially if the wind has died down.

When you sit at the base of Misery Hill and look to the west, you will see an unnamed peak that stands alone at an elevation of 13,384 feet. Just below the peak and down the long draw to the north is the Whitney Glacier. If you have the energy and the time, a short side trip to this peak is well worth the view of the biggest and longest glacier in

California. If you are not ready for a side trip (like most of us), you can also get an amazing view of the glacier from your next stop, the Summit Plateau.

While the name Misery Hill sounds extremely harsh, once you have climbed it, you will see the hill is not as harsh as its name implies. Climbing Misery Hill takes about 45 minutes

to an hour and is not too physically demanding except for the altitude gain which may be playing drum rolls inside your lungs. This area

A slow and steady pace gets you to the top of Misery Hill.

of the mountain is usually marked by a combination of brittle ice and volcanic rock. A slow steady pace brings you to the top of the hill and to the icy windswept Summit Plateau.

While climbing Misery Hill, you should concentrate on your breathing and try to establish some sort of rhythm. Because of the thinness of oxygen at this elevation, breathing patterns are extremely important. After inhaling a full breath to get all the oxygen you can into your lungs, you will need exhale fully and forcibly through pursed lips as if whistling. Doing this creates a slight back pressure allowing more oxygen into your lungs. Mountaineers refer to this breathing technique as Pressure Breathing. Breathing patterns at high altitudes are one of the many topics discussed in our basic mountaineering courses. Always keep a slow and steady pattern of breathing when climbing at high altitudes. You may find it beneficial to coordinate your footsteps with your breathing which helps you keep a steady rhythm.

Do not be afraid to turn around if you or anybody in your group experiences severe symptoms that seem to relate to mountain sickness such as vomiting and severe headaches. Going back down to lower elevations is the quickest way to relieve most symptoms you may have developed. Your safety and health are more important than reaching the Summit. There is a climber's motto that is important to remember: "It's just as important to know when to turn around, as it is to know when to go on." Remember, Mt. Shasta will be here longer than you will; you can try climbing it another day, so if you feel sick, do not push it.

To reach the Summit Plateau, you need to start your climb from the south side of Misery Hill. During the early climbing season there may be a trail of steps in the snow to follow; late in the season there will be a zigzag trail of footprints stomped into the loose talus. Due to the loose talus underfoot during the summer, you should use ski poles. However, on a snowfield you should always use your ice axe. After your slow and steady climb to the top of Misery Hill, you will reach a flat area called the Summit Plateau.

SUMMIT ICE FIELD

When you set foot on top of Misery Hill, you will also be taking your first step onto the Summit Plateau. This windswept Plateau, when snow covered, resembles a sea of snow which is sometimes called the Summit Ice Field. This expansive flat area sits at an elevation of 13,800 feet above sea level and offers some very spectacular views. The Plateau also provides a good resting spot for weary climbers before they start their last trek to the Summit.

Looking ahead to the north you can see two rocky pinnacles, which appear to be sculptured in ice, glistening in the early morning sun. A long time ago the pinnacle to the left was

Summit Plateau

known as McLean's Peak, but today it is referred to as the False Summit, and is sometimes climbed by those mistaking it for the true Summit. The pinnacle to the right was at one time called Muir Peak, named after John Muir, and is, indeed, Mt. Shasta's true Summit.

Before you make your final ascent to the Summit pinnacle, you should consider the spectacular views seen from the edges of the Plateau. The west edge offers a superb view of Shastina, Mt. Shasta's western-most flank peak. Its pinnacle rises 12,330 feet above sea level; Shastina can almost be called a mountain of its own since it has its own Summit. Shastina's immense crater holds a small lake inside which is named Clarence King Lake. Clarence King was a writer and a member of the U.S. Geological Exploration team, who was credited for discovering the glaciers on the north side of the mountain in the late 1800s. He was himself an accomplish mountaineer with many first ascents in the Sierra Nevada to the south including Mount Tyndall at 14,018 ft. Sisson Lake is located outside the main crater and inside the saddle between Shasta and Shastina. The lake is named after L. M. Sisson, for whom the city of Mount Shasta was originally named. In the summer, the lake is usually half-frozen and blue in color and is plainly visible from the Summit Plateau. Below the saddle the Whitney Glacier can be seen winding down the east slope of Shastina.

For one of the most impressive scenes on Mt. Shasta, take a quick stroll to the east side of the Plateau. Looking down the east slope of the mountain and to the south, you can see a deep gully called Mud Creek Canyon. The upper part of the canyon holds in its grip one of Mt. Shasta's smallest glaciers, the Mud Creek Glacier. This canyon is the largest, deepest, and oldest of the canyons on the mountain. In the past, there have been tremendous mud slides that have sent mud and water raging down the canyon, eventually emptying into the valley below. The town of McCloud can also be seen below Mud Creek along with a panoramic view of the flat, timbered valley known to the locals as the "McCloud Flats."

THE SMELL OF SULPHUR

While you are resting on the Summit Plateau, you may notice a foul smell of sulphur in the air emanating from the north. When you are ready to hike across the Plateau, you can follow the smell which will lead you directly between the two icy pinnacles. Hiking across this Plateau can be slow because of the altitude, but it's flat, a comforting relief after the climb up from the Red Banks.

One of the small Sulphur Springs that may have kept John Muir alive!

Nestled in a wind-protected area between the two pinnacles are the famous Sulphur Springs. They are famous because the well-known author and naturalist John Muir once spent the night there. John Muir and his partner Jerome Fay, a hardy and competent mountaineer, were caught on the Summit in a fierce early summer snow storm in 1877. With howling winds and darkness upon them, Muir concluded the only way to stay alive without descending was to lie in the hot pockets of mud and gravel. The hot pockets of mineral water are not very deep, and Muir could not fully immerse his almost frozen body in one. When the mineral water got too unbearably hot, the two would stand up and brave the violent winds, thinking they faced certain death.

In *Harper's New Monthly Magazine* of September 1877, John Muir writes,

"We lay flat on our backs, so as to present as little surface as possible to the wind. The mealy snow gathered on our breasts, and I did not rise again to my feet for seventeen hours. We were glad at first to see the snow drifting into the hollows of our clothing, hoping it would serve to deaden the force of the ice wind; but, though soft at first, it soon froze into a stiff, crusty heap, rather augmenting our novel misery."

They did survive, of course, even though their clothing was saturated with sulphur water and melting snow.

In the late 1800s, a copper monument was built by government employees of the United States Coast and Geodetic Survey for use as a signal tower for establishing a fixed point for their West Coast surveys. The monument also acted as a marker for climbers to assure them that they were ascending the right pinnacle. The copper monument, now gone, was placed on the Summit near where the record box is now located. It is no wonder that the monument is gone since few structures can withstand the fierce winds blowing across Shasta's Summit. Originally, there was a copper record box as well, now gone, which the climbers used to sign their names. The present record box was placed on the Summit by the Sierra Club Foundation. The registry book is located inside the box and is replaced by the Forest Service when the book is full.

ALMOST TO THE TOP

From the smelly Sulphur Springs to Mt. Shasta's top is a

Climbing the last several hundred feet to the Summit.

strenuous but short climb of several hundred feet. You will need to ascend the west side of the Summit pinnacle. When free of snow, a trail imprinted in the talus wraps around the pinnacle to the north and leads to a saddle between the North and South Summits. The pinnacle is fairly steep and you need to be aware of possible rock fall from above. Taking a right at the saddle will lead you to Shasta's Summit at 14,179 feet.

So after taking that right turn and following the path till it ends you are at the Summit. Yeah! Finally, with what little breath you have left, you can scream out and say "I made it," or dance a jig, or just crack a big smile and contemplate the breathtaking views. There is an excellent spot to rest with a rock backrest, and wind protection, next to the record box. Be sure to sign your name in the registry book located inside the record box. There is a pen in the box which you may have to thaw in order to write.

W. B. Beem standing. Tom Watson seated Miss Alice Cousins on her thirsty horse, Old Jump Up.

Photo courtesy of Siskiyou County Museum, Yreka, California

When you are standing on the Summit and thinking about the grueling climb you have just completed, imagine yourself doing it on horseback. In the late summer of 1903, Alice Cousins, guided by Tom Watson, rode her horse "Old Jump Up" to the Summit. This was the first horse to reach the Summit, but not the first animal. In 1883 Gilbert Thompson, a geographer with the U.S. Geological Survey, and local guide Tom Watson took two mules, illustriously named Dynamite and Croppy, to the top of Mt. Shasta. These mules and riders were guided by members of the survey team that had reached the Summit from the McCloud side, presently known as the Clear Creek route.

In years past, there were no restrictions on animals climbing the Summit; however, times have changed and dogs and other domesticated animals are not allowed in the Wilderness Area. Domesticated animals have the potential to disturb wildlife, destroy fragile vegetation, and affect other visitors' experiences.

THE SUMMIT

"When you're standing on the Summit, just crack a big smile and say, I made it. "

BREATHTAKING VIEWS

The views from the Summit of Mt. Shasta are similar as the

views from the Summit Plateau with the exception of those views down the steep east side of the Summit pinnacle. A topographical map will help

Summit Pinnacle 14,179 ft. early season.

115

you identify the glaciers, canyons, and some of the other landmarks. Looking to the east and down the mountain, you can see Shasta's fourth largest glacier, the Wintun Glacier. The glacier was named after the Wintun Indians who used to reside in the Mt. Shasta area. The upper glacier starts out wide and eventually winds downhill into the steep and narrow Ash Creek Canyon. If you look to the east - northeast, in the distance you can see the blue waters of Medicine Lake, one of the Cascade's shield volcanoes and the largest volcano by volume. A shield volcano is built up of countless outpourings of lava which slowly spread out and develop a broad, gently sloping cone with a flat, domical shape.

To the southeast is Mt. Lassen, the southernmost volcano in the Cascade Range. This snow-capped mountain, at 10,457 feet, may be smaller than Mt. Shasta, but it holds the title for being the world's largest plugged-dome volcano. Lassen is still considered active with some fumaroles and boiling mud pots reminding us of its recent eruption in 1915.

Looking due south under a cap of haze or smog, you will see the upper Sacramento Valley. The towns of Redding and Red Bluff are stretched out over the north end of the valley. Sometimes, when the sky is not too hazy, a short range of hills called the Sutter Buttes can be seen near the town of Sacramento. The Sutter Buttes are sometimes referred to as the world's smallest mountain range. The snowcapped mountain range called the Yolla Bollys can be seen on the west side of Sacramento Valley as well as Burney Mountain and Big Valley on the east side. Looking to the west of the Summit gives you a tremendous view of the Trinity Alps and the Eddy Mountain along with California's Coastal Range in the background.

A side trip to the north end of the Summit pinnacle is essential for some superb views of Shasta's second largest glacier, the Hotlum glacier. The Bolam glacier, the third largest glacier, can also be seen between Hotlum and Whitney glaciers. To get to the north end of the pinnacle, follow the path that you came in on to the point where you made a right turn. Keep going straight at this point and follow the path for a short distance until it ends at the North pinnacle.

Looking to the north, you can view a short range of mountains that lead into the Oregon Cascades. On the west side of the range is Shasta Valley with Interstate 5 passing through the towns of Weed and Yreka and heading in an almost straight line on its way to Oregon. To the northeast, Highway 97 can be seen winding through Mt. Shasta's lava flows, Grass Lake, and Butte Valley on its way to the Oregon border. If you have a clear day with perfect visibility, you can see some of the snowcapped tops of the Cascade volcanoes in the state of Oregon. Mt. McLoughlin, at 9,495 feet, happens to be Mt. Shasta's northerly neighbor in Oregon and is almost always visible from the Summit. If you are fortunate to Summit on a very bright and clear day you might just get really lucky and see some of the other volcanoes in the Oregon Cascade range such as the Three Sisters, Bachelor, or even Mt. Jefferson.

The views from the Summit are so rewarding that they will stick in your memory for the rest of your life. Having a camera and a good battery, gives you the chance to capture

View from the Summit Pinnacle, looking back down the Avalanche Gulch Route with the Mt. Whitney Glacier to the right.

these special moments in time so you can share them with family and friends. If you have cell reception you could even take a photo and Facebook all you friends right there on the

Summit! A small pair of binoculars can also be an asset, giving you a closer view of the canyons and glaciers that are part of Mt. Shasta's slopes.

THE DESCENT

"Ascending is optional while Descending is Mandatory."

CLIMBING DOWN THE MOUNTAIN

After spending some time on the Summit, the decision has to be made to leave to make the second half of your journey. This is usually the hardest decision of your trip because of the struggle it took to get to the top. You may feel like you have been sentenced by a judge and jury, and the overwhelming verdict is you must descend or die. The self-discipline needed to climb down the Mountain is as important as the self-discipline needed to get to the top. There is a saying in mountaineering that is very relevant here "While getting to the top is optional, getting down is mandatory!" Your trip down the Mountain requires you not only to return to base camp, but also to pack up and carry your heavy pack downhill while trying to reach the Bunny Flat parking lot before nightfall. Oftentimes climbers who spend too much time on the Summit will develop some form of altitude sickness, headaches, or maybe just a general feeling of weakness. We suggest only staying on the Summit no more than 15 to 30 minutes, less if it is very crowded. Do not let this uncomfortable feeling scare you; a quick descent will almost always lead to a noticeable improvement. Sometimes headaches can occur while descending, and the best cure is to drink plenty of water, providing you have some left.

YOU HAVE TO DESCEND NOW

The descent of Avalanche Gulch is pretty straightforward; you just follow your line of ascent. Descending with an ice axe is a must unless the ground is free of snow, in which case ski poles can be used. Once you return to Sulphur Springs, you should travel across the Plateau the same way that you came in.

The descent is effortless on your lungs, but it can be hard on your body, especially on someone who has weak knees or ankles. An athletic wrap or brace should be worn on any part of your body you think may give you difficulty.

A good way to estimate your return climb is to check your time going up and cut it in half. Although this is not strictly accurate, it can provide you with a very close estimate. When traveling down the Mountain, you should follow the very same pathway you used when you came up. The one place on the route where there might be an exception to this rule might be when you are going through the Red Banks. If the chutes are still very icy and you feel uncomfortable going down them then you can always traverse over towards Thumb Rock, being aware, of course, of the dangers of the Konwakiton bergschrund. Once you reach the saddle between the Red Banks and Thumb Rock then it is a straight shot down towards The Heart. Conservation of time and energy is valuable on your descent; neither one can you afford to waste.

Descending the Mountain will give you a totally different experience than what you had on your way up. You will know in your mind that you have already reached the Summit and any obstacles you may face going down may well be inconsequential, but never forget that dangers such as rock fall and fatigue still exist so never let your guard down.

You may have heard the term "Glissading," that is sliding down a slope of ice or snow in control, with the emphasis on the word "control." Glissading down the Mountain will have as much impact on your memory as when you took your first step onto the Summit pinnacle. It can be a fun way to make a quick descent down the Mountain; however, the snow conditions have to be just right for a comfortable glissade. If they are not, you may find yourself walking back to base camp or worse yet getting a helicopter ride off the mountain because you broke an ankle or some other part of your body due to an uncontrolled fall. Glissading will be discussed in more detail later, but remember that we see more accidents due to glissading than any other hazard.

If you made your climb during the early morning hours, your Summit descent will probably be between the hours of 11:00 a.m. and 2:00 p.m. During these hours, the snow tends to soften and accumulate on the bottom of your crampons (balling up) causing you to lose traction. When these conditions exist, you need to remove your crampons. If the snow is still frozen, you will need to descend with your crampons on. Always use your ice axe when descending, regardless of the condition of the snow.

Walking down Misery Hill should be approached with caution and not with the eagerness to be the first climber off the Mountain. When the ground is free of snow, ski poles are helpful for stability and support on the loose volcanic talus. Misery Hill, when snow covered, can be glissaded down, but only on the southwest side of the hill. The south side where you walked up will usually be crusted over with ice because of the fierce winds that blow across its slopes, making it impossible to glissade. Many climbers start their glissade above the main chute of the Red Banks. We highly discourage this because the chute gets quite steep and usually stays icy much longer than the surrounding snow fields. There are also usually other climbers coming up this chute and if you glissade down it there is the chance you will run into them and the chances for injury are very high. So please do not be that "idiot" who comes screaming down the main chute completely out of control and hurts someone. We suggest down climbing one of the chutes and then begin you glissade below the Red Banks.

The glissading chute runs downhill below the Red Banks and passes by The Heart, sometimes leading as far down as Helen Lake. A glissading chute is no more than a trail created by climbers sliding downhill on the seat of their pants. Sometimes this chute can get several feet deep and for all appearance looks like a Luge run with banking turns and drops. With the right type of snow conditions, you can glissade back to Helen Lake in less than 30 minutes! This is obviously much quicker than the original time it took to climb from Helen Lake up to the Red Banks. Glissading down from just below the Red Banks should not be done without the knowledge of self-arrest techniques. Poor knowledge or incorrect use of such techniques can lead to a devastating, involuntary, and uncontrolled slide down the Mountain and has resulted in past fatalities.

The best time of year for glissading is late spring through early to mid summer. In late summer the snow becomes sun-cupped, a condition that occurs when the snow on or under the surface begins to thaw; this is the final process before it melts. Glissading on sun-cupped conditions can be done; however, climbers usually will wear an agonizing hole in the seat of their pants and their backs will hurt from all the jarring caused by the uneven snow surface.

One last important thing to know before glissading is to wear the proper clothing. If you have any open skin showing, you can incur severe ice burns. You need to wear gloves with grips, a long-sleeved shirt, and some type of rear protection like maybe a pair of heavy surfing shorts. Some climbers take a strong plastic bag and wear it like a diaper, thus protecting their pants and rump, but we find that the plastic usually does not hold up for very long. If you do decide to try the plastic bags please be sure to pick them up and throw them away when you reach the trailhead.

Another option would be to wear rain gear, with your long johns underneath and a thick pair of shorts. A third option we have discovered is to go to your local hardware store and buy some Tool Dip which is used to dip the handles of pliers and other such tools to provide additional grip. Take the tool dip and slather it all over the rear end of your rain pants. This works great for protecting your expensive Gore-Tex™ pants plus it will make your pants fast like lightening! You should also wear gaiters to keep the snow from creeping up your pants leg and down your boots. If glissading sounds too boring for you and you are thinking about taking a saucer down, forget it, as that would be pure suicide! We would probably end up scraping you off a rock.

GET READY TO GLISSADE

The first thing to do before starting a glissade is to sit down and remove your crampons. Remember that as soon as you take them off you might slide so be prepared. **NEVER, EVER GLISSADE WITH CRAMPONS ON UNLESS YOU WANT A RIDE IN A HELICOPTER WITH A DISLOCATED OR BROKEN ANKLE OR WORSE!** Glissading with crampons on can allow many types of accidents to occur such as: glissading into another climber and cutting their back or arms open, snagging your gaiters or pants and cutting yourself, your crampons popping off and cutting either you or someone else, or worse of all catching a crampon point in a firm section of snow or ice resulting in a broken ankle or worse yet a complete ankle dislocation (we have seen this happen!

The standard posture is to sit fairly erect, with your knees slightly bent and your legs stretched out in front of you. Balancing your weight out is good for speed and stability. You should grip your ice axe in whichever hand is most comfortable using the proper self-arrest technique with your thumb under the adze and the rest of your hand wrapped around the head of the axe. As an example, let's say you will be using your right hand as the brake hand. First hold the ice axe by the shaft near the spike with your right hand, then lay the axe along the right side of your body, while still in a sitting position. Make sure the pick of the axe is facing away from you. Your second step is to reach across your body with your left hand, palm up and place the head of the ice axe in your open palm with your thumb hooking under the adze. Then wrap your hand around the head of the axe as described above. This is the basic self-arrest grip, only you are doing it while in the sitting position.

Chances are other climbers will be glissading in front of you and behind you so it is a good idea to practice braking both with the spike of the ice axe and also using the self-arrest technique. To brake with the spike just lever up with your left hand while keeping your right hand by your right hip. It also helps to spread your legs apart and gather snow between them as well as using your heels to slow yourself down.

When all else fails then you will need to roll over onto your stomach and use the self-arrest technique of digging the pick into the snow while levering up with the spike. Never drag the pick or adze through the snow while in the sitting position because you will invariably catch them on some harder snow and goodbye ice axe! Then you are in some real trouble flying down the mountain with no ice axe and therefore no way to slow yourself down. Once you are comfortable slowing yourself down, then just let go and enjoy the ride. Reaching speeds of 20 mph is common, but your backside will most likely complain of the high speeds eventually. This part of the climb is definitely the highlight of the trip for many of our clients, but remember always stay in control because when things go wrong, they go wrong fast and you are still high up on a big mountain. If you would like to become really proficient at glissading or if the above instructions seem too complicated then we highly recommend taking our one day, basic ice axe and crampon clinic before your climb. You will gain the experience and knowledge needed to properly climb up Mt. Shasta and then glissade down safely using the proper self-arrest technique.

If the snow conditions are not favorable for glissading (too firm), then you will be forced to walk down from the Red Banks. When walking down a steep snowfield, the climber has to be familiar with the proper technique for using an ice axe. The technique for going down is determined by the hardness and angle of the snow. The plunge step is the most common and most aggressive step used while descending, but only really works on softer snow so more than likely you would be glissading. You will want to keep your knee's slightly bent, face outward down the mountain, and step aggressively away from the slope and land solidly on your heel. Always make sure you dig your heel in with each step to ensure solid footing and to avoid an unplanned glissade. Flat footing is another method used to descend, but only on firm snow. The object here is to keep you feet spread apart and your feet flat so that when you step down all the crampon points come into contact with the firm snow at the same time. Crampons are a must while descending on consolidated or frozen snow. Be especially careful not to step on your gaiters or your boots with crampons on since this can cause you to trip and fall as well as rip a hole in your expensive gaiters or Gore Tex™ pants.

Your crampons should be removed if you are descending on soft powder or slushy snow. Once again, the ice axe should be held using the self-arrest grip. You can alternate hands, but always keep the pick of the axe facing uphill (behind you). If a fall should occur, then you can go immediately into the self-arrest technique. Try using the same walking technique as the plunge step, only this time keep your body in a crouched position with your feet and ice axe firmly planted in front.

Rock fall threats still exist during the afternoon hours, but it is generally not as dangerous to the climber as in the morning. The softening snow in the afternoon catches the smaller rocks and keeps them from rolling too far down the Gulch. Most of the smaller avalanches occur in the afternoon beneath the upper part of Casaval Ridge. Whether you decide to climb down or glissade, always keep in mind that avalanches and rock fall can occur at any time so **ALWAYS WEAR YOUR HELMET**.

SKI DESCENTS

Rarely do people actually ski or ride from the true Summit of

Mt. Shasta due to the icy and windblown nature of the upper mountain snow. In the summer months it seems that most riders leave their skis at the top of Short Hill/Base of Misery. In the event that conditions are good enough, the best choice is to retrace your ascent route back to the base of Misery Hill. From this point you have a couple of options for good riding.

Skiing is usually best below 12,000 ft.

Above the Red Banks the best skiing is generally to the skier's right. This provides a longer steeper line free of climbers still ascending the route later in the day. Additionally this line receives the earliest sun so tends to be softer snow and better skiing.

In the event that this route is too steep or the line is just in poor condition, the second choice is to ski the ascent route near Thumb Rock. This line is generally icier and has the distinct disadvantage of having climbers still on the ascent well into the afternoon. Remember that it is good mountain etiquette not to ski directly above or near someone still climbing. The climber always has the right of way and it is your responsibility to yield to him or her.

Finally, in recent years more and more people have been trying to ski the chutes that run vertically through the Red Banks. THIS IS UNACCEPTABLE AND DANGEROUS!

These chutes are icy and rarely provide great skiing and they are difficult to see from above. There have been several near misses over the last few years from people attempting to ski the chutes while climbers are using them to ascend. In these situations the skier either collided with the climber or hit the side wall of the Red Banks. If you "must" ski these chutes make sure you move slowly through and that you can see down the entire route before entering. However, is just best to ski someplace else.

HELEN LAKE TO BUNNY FLAT

When you return to camp, your tent will be more than just a welcome sight. Your shorts may be ripped and your rear end wet and cold from your glissade through The Heart. If you glissaded without wearing gaiters, then likely your boots will be packed with snow and your socks sopping wet, and yesterday's blisters may be rubbed raw and possibly bleeding. Your legs also may be very sore and feel like a wet noodle with an occasionally throbbing muscle. Your face may feel as though it has been in a microwave oven because of the pulsating sun and fierce winds which have been pounding you for the last 8 to 10 hours. Your hunger pains may have taken control of your body, and your tongue may be starving for something wet besides snow. Your head may also be pounding from the heat and altitude, giving way to wishing you were already at the parking lot.

It's a welcome sight to see your camp after a successful summit climb.

Although you may feel uncomfortable, tired, and grouchy, you will also feel rewarded that you have made a successful ascent to the Summit and returned to camp safely. You will know in your heart and mind that you have succeeded in what you set out to accomplish: to stand on Mt. Shasta's Summit. You will have a sense of fulfillment even though your body may feel as though it has been on a roller coaster ride or run over by a large truck from your glissade down the mountain. You will be astonished at the mountaineering experience you have gained. You will also know that the hard part is over and that you can undertake any challenges left to get you back to your vehicle. If it helps at all you will forget all about the uncomfortable things once you are sitting in front of a cold drink and a slice of pizza back in town and more than likely planning your next trip up the mountain.

Getting yourself more comfortable will be the first thing you will want do when you arrive at base camp, if time allows. Getting out of your wet clothes and into some dry ones is a great idea. It is always a delight if you have left a quart of water in your tent or even saved a quart of juice from the day before. A hot meal and maybe a short nap will return the strength badly needed to get you off the mountain.

Be cautious here about taking too much time back at base camp. It is a bad idea to run out of daylight since you are extremely tired and if something goes wrong it gets worse very quickly.

The average hiking time back to the Horse Camp Cabin is around 2 hours from Helen Lake. The hike from the Cabin to the parking lot takes about an hour with no rest stops. That gives you about 3-4 hours hiking time to get you off the mountain. Allow yourself some extra time to rest at the Cabin and hydrate yourself with some of the mountain's pure spring water. If the snow conditions allow you might even be able to glissade some on your descent down to the Cabin. If that is the case you might want to leave your wet clothes on until you reach the Horse Camp. Keep in mind that glissading with a huge backpack on can be quite challenging, but the snow is usually quite soft by this time so just point your feet and go!

PACK OUT WHAT YOU PACKED IN

Here's the target for your pack out system!

Almost all climbers have a great respect for the outdoors and wilderness areas. Mt. Shasta, like any other wilderness, deserves respect since it is the mountain that has allowed you to climb to its Summit and camp on its slopes. The last thing the mountain wants to feel is trash blowing over its ridges and into its deep crevasses. Please be a respectful climber and pack out your trash, including even something as small as a gum wrapper and if you see someone leaving trash behind respectfully ask them to pick it up. We are all custodians of the Wilderness because it belongs to all of us. All human waste pack out bags should also go with you. Horse Camp has no trash facilities and the plastic bags should not be deposited in their toilets. Once you get back to the Bunny Flat parking lot there are separate trash receptacles for the human waste pack out bags and normal trash. If you packed it in, then PLEASE pack it out! Every year the wilderness ranger's end up carrying out thousands of pounds of excrement left behind by climbers who were not respectful enough of the Wilderness to carry out their own poop.

Snowshoes may be needed during the early climbing season when descending from Helen Lake to the parking lot. During the late spring, the snow changes from a frozen state in the morning to really soft and mushy in the afternoon. After the snow melts in the afternoon, it then refreezes during the night. As we move from late spring into mid-summer, the process of freezing and thawing only occurs in the top layers of the snowpack leaving the deeper layers in a somewhat frozen state. Couple this with other climbers compressing the snow and you have a very supportive snowpack as we move later into the climbing season. Traveling with a full pack and without snowshoes can often cause you to sink (post holing) up to your waist in snow, resulting in a very long and miserable hike down the mountain.

An ice axe can be used for the return trip down the mountain, however, ski poles are recommended since they offer excellent stabilization and support for descending in soft or sun-cupped snow and the loose volcanic talus.

After hiking down Standstill Hill and returning to 50/50 Flat, you will have a choice of which way to hike down to the Cabin. During the late summer months, the large hill right below 50/50 Flat is quicker than the Climbers Gully and there will already be a well-worn foot trail. When the ground is covered in snow, Climbers Gully is the best and fastest route to take. The Gully is located on the south side of the hill and offers a moderate descent to the Cabin.

When traveling downhill, always be courteous and give the uphill climber the right-of-way. Walking downhill can often cause your pack to sway from side to side, so be especially careful not to bump the uphill climber with your pack. Chances are your pack will not be packed as tightly as when you first started your climb the day before. Have you ever taken something out of a box and then could not fit it back in? That is what happens to some climbers when they leave Helen Lake. They just slop everything into their pack so they can get down the mountain in a hurry.

There are some personal items that need to be accessible for your trip out such as some extra clothing, food, water, and sunscreen. The afternoon sun on the mountain can be very intense, especially when it is reflected off the snow. Your sunglasses, preferably with side shields, should be worn at all times to avoid burning your eyes. Make sure to put on some sunscreen as well. If you are hiking close to dark, it's a good idea to have your flashlight or headlamp accessible in the top lid of your pack. Your gaiters can be a valuable asset when leaving Helen Lake because of the slushy snow. Gaiters also stop the loose talus from creeping down the inside of your boots. It may be too hot to wear your gloves, but keep them handy since the hike from the Cabin to the parking lot can sometimes hold some very cold pockets of air.

BACK AT THE CABIN

The Cabin is always a good place to rest before the final hike down to the parking lot. You may feel like you do not need to stop; however, the mountain's pure spring water will surely lure you there. Chances are there will be other climbers and day hikers resting at the Cabin and they usually will inquire about the conditions along the route to Helen Lake or the Summit. Get ready to answer the most famous question asked at the Cabin: "Did you go to the top?" It's very rewarding to say YES, and you may want to add the following: "I also withstood the 60-mile-an-hour-winds on Misery Hill."

The one-hour hike to the parking lot may be the easiest part of the climb, but it will also seem to be the longest. Your anticipation of arriving at the parking lot along with your sore shoulders from your heavy pack may make the parking lot seem 100 miles away. As for your headache and sore muscles, a few pain relievers and a good night's sleep will fix you right up. When you do reach the parking lot, tired and hungry, you will be able to turn around and look up at the mountain and reward yourself by smiling and saying, "I did it."

No one can ever conquer the mountain, but you can feel victorious for the climb that you have achieved. There will be times when the perils of nature will outwit you and your climb may not be successful. Sometimes there will be a danger of extreme rock fall or avalanches forcing you to turn back. At other times a storm will move in and the winds will be so high or the visibility so bad that you are forced to turn back. The most important factor to consider is the mental and physical challenges that you conquered on this climb. Sometimes you may just feel like taking a day hike and other times you may feel like climbing to the Summit.

Mountaineering is a very personal endeavor. It requires you to push yourself to the limits of your physical and mental abilities. Always remember that you can only conquer on foot what you feel you can conquer in your mind.

OTHER ROUTES ON MT. SHASTA

While avalanche gulch is by far the most popular route to reach the Summit of Mt. Shasta there are actually 17 established routes on the mountain. Some of these routes, such as the Clear Creek route, are actually considered "easier" than the Avalanche Gulch route while others, such as Casaval Ridge or the Hotlum Direct, are substantially more difficult and climbable for a much shorter span of time. In the following chapter we will describe the five most accessible climbs on the mountain that are beginner to intermediate in climbing level depending, of course, on the time of year that you are attempting to climb.

WEST FACE

GETTING THERE

Both the West Face route and the Casaval Ridge route are accessed from the Bunny Flat trailhead. This is the same trailhead as used for the Avalanche Gulch route described in detail in the previous chapter.

HITTING THE TRAIL

Starting from the Bunny Flats Trailhead, start hiking along the Avalanche Gulch trail until you reach the Sierra Club Cabin at Horse Camp.

At this point you will break off to the trail behind the cabin trending to the northwest. In the early season when snow is on the ground this trail is often marked by wands. This trail breaks up the hill behind the cabin through a grove of Shasta Red fir and to the west of Casaval Ridge. From the top of the first rise the trail continues to trend to the left below a popular local ski spot called Giddy-Giddy Gulch. The trail then continues to work its way around to the west crossing a series of ridges and gullies.

When traversing in the winter, spring, or even early summer season it is important to be aware of the avalanche conditions. Though these gullies look like benign snow slopes instead of avalanche slide paths, upon closer inspection the trees in the middle of the slopes are mangled and lay flat because of the force of the avalanches that come crashing down throughout the winter. Even the trees at the edges of the gullies have "flagging" where the tree's uphill branches and bark have been torn off by the immense forces of these avalanches. In bad conditions these gullies can become the deadliest of terrain traps.

The trail continues over one last ridge of smaller shrubby vegetation that is usually wind scoured through the season. From here the final slope is accessed that leads to Hidden Valley. Much like the gullies leading up to this point, this slope can be avalanche prone and is steep enough for a sustained fall. Once negotiated with proper techniques the area ahead opens up into broad flat area framed by Shastina and the 4,000 foot West Face.

This broad open area is known as "Hidden Valley" the primary base camp area for West Face ascents. As it is fairly level and later in the season, it has a water source in the form of a stream running through it. The areas above Hidden Valley have steep slopes, offer no protection from wind, avalanches and rock fall. Most climbers choose to stop here in Hidden Valley because of the poor selection of base camps up higher.

THE CLIMB

The route starts at the far end of Hidden Valley in a steep snow gully between two large outcroppings. With a slope angle nearing 45° the crux of the climb is often here, especially when it is icy. Due to its western aspect, this route often gets baked by late afternoon sun and is one of the last features on the mountain to receive

Base Camp below the West Face of Mt. Shasta.

morning sunlight. Thus, icy conditions persist during morning climbs in the summer. These icy sections, particularly this lowest gulley, have been the sight of several falls and injuries throughout the years.

Once the initial crux has been negotiated, the couloir opens onto a broader face and the slope angle eases back to between 30° and 40°. The climb moves past a few islands of talus all the while angling for a saddle of snow in the band of reddish rock at the top of the face. Though rock fall is less of a hazard on the West Face as other routes, such as Avalanche Gulch, it does happen from time to time and this was the sight of a rock fall fatality in 2010.

Towards the top of the West Face the slope angle steepens once again into almost a small bowl that tops out into a ridge. To the right a large red rock formation marks the junction of the West Face with Casaval Ridge and the Whitney Cirque. From the top of this feature all of West Face and Casaval Ridge is visible. To the southeast is Avalanche Gulch. To the north is the Whitney Glacier separating Shastina from the Summit Plateau of Mt. Shasta. Traversing to the east and descending slightly is the base of Misery Hill. From here you follow the Avalanche Gulch route description to the Summit.

SKI DESCENTS

Most skiers attempting the West Face usually start their descent from the top of the face rather from the Summit itself. This saves transitioning and hiking back up hill from Misery to the top of the West Face. Since the West Face receives sunlight later in the day it is likely to turn to corn snow. When it does finally soften up though its long consistent open face makes for one of the most classic ski descents on the mountain.

ROUTE NOTES

Two points of caution on descending the West Face include watching not to get drawn into the wrong descent gullies. Towards the bottom of the West Face are a series of chutes that rock out. It isn't wise to descend without having inspected the route on the way up. Finally, the couloir above Hidden Valley can present a hazard as it is often still icy later in the day and climbers can still be on the route. Skiing or riding through this section without first visualizing the route can place yourself and others in serious danger.

SECTION ELEVATION GAIN TIME

Bunny Flat to Horse Camp	6,860 ft to 7,880 ft	1,020 ft	1-2 hours
Horse Camp to Hidden Valley	7,880 ft to 9,300 ft	1,420 ft	3-4 hours
Hidden Valley to Top of West Face	9,300 ft to 13,390 ft	4,090 ft	5-7 hours
Top of West Face to Top of Misery Hill	13,390 ft to 13,800 ft	410 ft	<1 hour
Top of Misery Hill to Summit	13,800 ft to 14,179 ft	379 ft	1 hour

CASAVAL RIDGE
INTERMEDIATE ROUTE

Casaval Ridge is the strikingly beautiful ridge which forms the western/northwestern boundary to Avalanche Gulch. This route is considered by some to be one of the longest and most aesthetic lines on the mountain. While the above mentioned routes are climbed mostly in the summer and fall months Casaval Ridge is almost always climbed in the winter through early summer. By the time we are well into summer this route gets very rocky and icy and therefore quite dangerous.

GETTING THERE

Both the West Face route and the Casaval Ridge route are accessed from the Bunny Flat trailhead. This is the same trailhead as used for the Avalanche Gulch route described in detail in the previous chapters.

HITTING THE TRAIL

From the Sierra Club Cabin at Horse Camp one starts out on the same trail leading to the West Face. This trail gains the ridge just a few minutes from the cabin where it opens up onto a broad step just above the Cabin. Breaking off to the right of the West Face trail you can either follow the ridge directly up or veer a bit to the left and ascend up a small gully called Giddy-Giddy Gulch. Either way you will top out at 9,800 feet at a beautiful camping site in a small saddle. Due to the number of gendarmes (rocky spires protruding from the ridge) there are not many places to establish a camp on the ridge. This small saddle offers a popular spot with some protection from the wind.

THE CLIMB

From here, climb up to the left and gain the main Casaval Ridge. The ridge is fairly flat at this point, but after ascending 300 feet or so the route will drop down about 50 feet and then start ascending and traversing around several towers

which most climber's prefer to climb on climbers left or the northwest side. The route will definitely start to steepen at this point to 45-55 degrees depending on the snow drifts. At 10,800 feet

Climber high on the Casaval Ridge Route.

you will come to the "first window" which allows for some great views into Avalanche Gulch and is also an escape route onto the easier slopes into the Gulch. Be aware of the possible avalanche danger when using this as a descent.

The route continues to traverse the ridge, a bit steeper in sections until you get to the "second window." An escape route exists if you traverse to the northwest and join the broad West Face route. Again, be aware of the avalanche potential of both traversing northwest and the West Face avalanche conditions. Working past the second window you have about 1,300 ft of climbing before eventually topping out above the Trinity Chutes via the "Catwalk." A narrow walkway connecting Casaval Ridge to the sub-plateau just west of the base of Misery Hill at 13,100 ft. Finally you join the Avalanche Gulch route for the final 1,079 ft. to the Summit.

DESCENDING

For the descent you can either follow the Avalanche Gulch route down or descend the way you came up. A note of warning for those who decide to descend Avalanche Gulch. If your camp is at 9,800 feet on Casaval Ridge the traverse can be brutal if the sun has baked those slopes out of Helen Lake.

SKIING DESCENTS

Although Casaval Ridge does not lend itself to skiing directly it does provide some excellent options for ski access. Many locals will use this ridge to access shorter day tours that drop back into Avalanche Gulch. Any number of lines back up to the "First Window" offer short steeper descents. In addition to these lines, skiing back toward the ascent route into Giddy-Giddy Gulch gives this area a variety of terrain to ski from many differing aspects.

Once at the top of Casaval Ridge, one can move to the southeast to find the top of the Trinity Chutes. These long tight steep chutes offer some of the toughest skiing on the mountain and should only be attempted by the most skilled of ski mountaineers. A fall in this area could mean serious injury or death. Depending on the snow pack, some of these chutes have been known to require a short rappel. Keep in mind that any rock fall or avalanches started here may also hit climbers in the gulch below. When done safely though, these chutes can offer some of the most challenging and rewarding ski lines on the mountain.

SECTION ELEVATION GAIN TIME

SECTION	ELEVATION	GAIN	TIME
Bunny Flat to Horse Camp	6,860 ft to 7,880 ft	1,020 ft	1-2 hours
Horse Camp to Base Camp	7,880 ft to 9,800 ft	1,920 ft	3-4 hours
Base Camp to First Window	9,800 ft to 10,800 ft	1,000 ft.	2-4 hours
First Window to Second Window	10,800 ft to 11,800 ft	1,000 ft	1-2 hours
Second Window to Catwalk	11,800 ft to 13,100 ft	1,300 ft	2-3 hours
Catwalk to Top of Misery Hill	13,100 ft to 13,800 ft	700 ft	1-2 hours
Top of Misery Hill to Summit	13,800 ft to 14,179 ft	379 ft	1 hour

CLEAR CREEK
Beginner Route

GETTING THERE

Clear Creek Trailhead (6,800 feet) is reached from the town of McCloud. Drive east on Highway 89 for 2.8 miles to Pilgrim Creek Road (Road 13), you will see a sign that says Mt. Shasta Wilderness; turn to your left and follow that road for 5.2 miles. Then turn left on Widow Springs Road and proceed 5 miles to the junction of McKenzie Butte Road (Road 31). Cross the McKenzie Butte Road and follow the Clear Creek Trailhead sign approximately 2.5 miles to the trailhead. Also watch for big Mule deer (Bucks) that inhabit that area. You can take a more scenic route by taking the Ski Park Highway north of Highway 89 until you run into the #31 Road. The #31 Road takes you around the east side of the mountain, crossing Squaw and Mud Creeks, for 11.5 miles until you reach the intersection of #41N15 and #41N61. Watch closely for the Clear Creek Trailhead sign. This way is more complex and we recommend that you refer to a Shasta Trinity National Forest Service road map. The following Routes can be reached from this Trailhead: Clear Creek, Wintun Ridge, and Konwakiton Glacier (from the east).

HITTING THE TRAIL

Considered by most to be the easiest of the all the routes on Mt. Shasta, Clear Creek can still be quite challenging. This route is accessed from the Clear Creek trailhead, on the SE side of the mountain. After leaving the trailhead the trail meanders through pine forest until it finally comes out of the trees and begins to follow the east rim of Mud Creek. The views from here are spectacular indeed! The main base camp area is around 8,400 feet where the trail crosses a stream whose sources are right above you. Make sure you camp at least 100 feet from the stream. There are some good camp sites past the stream and up the hill about 100 yards or so.

THE CLIMB

From base camp the route takes you up and bit more to the west before heading straight up. Be aware that there are many trails through the talus so it is best to just find one that seems to be moving up and veering ever so slightly more towards the right sky line. At approximately 12,800 feet, there is a pile of rocks which resemble a mushroom and is therefore called... Mushroom Rock. It is a rather distinctive looking landmark so be sure to keep an eye out for it. It is really not all that big, maybe 8-12 feet high.

From here you have two choices: you can either climb straight up through some steep bands of loose rock or veer off to the right a bit and climb around the steeper rock bands. The second choice is the most popular, but quite often there is a snow field that has to be dealt with as soon as you turn the corner. This generally is not a problem if you brought crampons and an ice axe, but if not then it can be far more challenging. Once this obstacle has been surmounted, then it is a quick hike up some easy talus to the broad Summit plateau just west of the Summit pinnacle where it joins the Avalanche Gulch route.

DESCENDING

The descent is the same as the ascent. We have found that the average time to climb this route is 5-7 hours with 3-4 hours for the descent back to base camp.

SKIING DESCENTS

Though Clear Creek has great open low angle terrain it is rarely skied. The Southeast facing aspect of this route lends itself to more direct sunlight than many of the other routes on the mountain. This means that much of the terrain is melted out and free of snow by the time the trailhead is open to foot traffic. The East Face tends to offer a better ski descent from this side.

ROUTE NOTES

Some things to keep in mind when climbing this route. The dust and wind can be horrendous so clear goggles are very nice to have before the sun comes up. Make sure you keep moving to the right or else you might end up in the Mud Creek drainage which can be downright unpleasant all the way to quite possibly being deadly. This is doubly important on your descent. It is imperative that you keep to the left and stay out of that drainage.

A map and compass could be a life saver in whiteout conditions, but of course, we highly recommend not climbing in a whiteout. Case in point there was a fatality in spring of 2011 on this very route due to two climbers getting lost in a snow storm and veering too far to the right and dropping into the Mud Creek drainage!

SECTION ELEVATION GAIN TIME

Clear Creek Trailhead to Base Camp	6,800 ft to 8,400 ft	1,600 ft	3 hours
Base Camp to Mushroom Rock	8,400 ft to 12,800 ft	4,400 ft	3-5 hours
Mushroom Rock to Summit	12,800 ft to 14,179 ft	1,379 ft	2-3 hours

HOTLUM BOLUM RIDGE
INTERMEDIATE ROUTE

GETTING THERE

To get to the North Gate Trailhead (6,920 feet) from the town of Mt. Shasta, drive north on I-5 to the City of Weed. Then take Highway 97 north toward Oregon driving though Shasta's ancient lava flows. After about 30 minutes of driving and 14.5 miles from Weed, turn right on Military Pass Road (Road 43N19). This road served as an old emigrant trail and as early as 1853 wagon trains of overland emigrants crossed the M.P. road into Shasta Valley and Yreka. Turn right and drive 4.5 miles to the junction of the Andesite Logging Road and stay right. From this point, just follow the signs to the Northgate trailhead. There is a small dirt parking area next to an old logging clear cut along with a restroom and a fee tube.

HITTING THE TRAIL

The trail begins at an elevation of 6,920 feet and meanders for some time in a forest of Shasta Red firs before it eventually opens up into a forest of White Bark pines. One area in particular is quite easy to identify and that is an area that has hundreds of these trees laid out flat by an avalanche that occurred off of the slope to the south back in 1997.

The trail continues west from here and contours around the slopes to the south and eventually heads to the south. At this point the trail will really begin to climb up into a broad, rocky valley. At around 9,500 feet in elevation you will begin to see tent sites on the west side of a running creek. This is the most popular area to make a base camp for a Summit bid. Another option for camping is found by continuing straight up from the White Bark pines blow down and ascending the north facing slope. When you gain the top of this slope, a fairly flat and broad mesa will be in front of you. There are literally hundreds of beautiful areas to camp on numerous benches up here on the Mesa. This is the best area to camp in the early season when there is still snow on the slopes directly above the White Bark pines, otherwise these slopes can be very unpleasant to climb without snow so we suggest going to the first base camp area mentioned.

THE CLIMB

The route itself follows large/broad snowfields up to 12,000

Looking up the Hotlum Bolum Ridge route from Base Camp.

feet where an obvious "ramp" will take you another 1,000 feet to the flat area known as "the Step" at 12,900 feet. The bottom of the ramp has a very large crevasse known as the Carnivorous Bergshrund which can be circumvented by going to the west or climbers right this crevasse has seen several climbers enter its maw uninvited over the years.

Once on the Step, the route continues straight up a triangular snowfield and passes to the right of the Rabbit

Ears which are two very prominent rock towers. Once past these two features, look to traverse to the west via a notch which leads into a gully called the "Bowling Alley." At this point it is a short climb to the top of the Alley and from here head straight up the scree/talus slopes and top out onto the north Summit of Mt. Shasta. From here it is a quick traverse to the southwest and a short climb to the actual high point of Mt. Shasta. Well done indeed!

DESCENDING

The descent is the same as the ascent. We have found the average time to climb this route is about 8-9 hours with about 3-4 hours for the descent.

SKIING DESCENTS

Skiing the Hotlum-Bolum Ridge is not recommended. The upper portions of the route tend to have thin cover making finding a clean descent tricky. Once on the ridge proper the route can be icy and a fall could end with a skier in a crevasse. Skiing on and around glaciers should be reserved for only the best and most experienced of ski mountaineers.

SECTION ELEVATION GAIN TIME

Northgate Trailhead to Base Camp	6,920 ft to 9,500 ft	2,580 ft	3-5 hours
Base Camp to Foot of Ramp	9,500 ft to 12,000 ft	2,500 ft	2-4 hours
Foot of Ramp to Rabbit Ears	12,000 ft to 13,500 ft	1,500 ft	2-4 hours
Rabbit Ears to Summit	13,500 ft to 14,179 ft	679 ft	1-3 hours

HOTLUM WINTUN ROUTE
INTERMEDIATE ROUTE

While one of the more remote routes on the mountain, the Hotlum/Wintun ridge sees a fair number of climbers especially later in the season which could partially be due to the fact that the Brewer Creek trailhead is the last trailhead on the mountain to melt out and become accessible by vehicle. This route is also considered by many to be the best skiing line on the mountain with many lucky skiers able to get over 7,000 vertical in on one run!

Brewer Creek trailhead, depending on the past winters snowfall, melts out usually sometime from early to mid July. Always call ahead to the Mt. Shasta Ranger Station to find out the status of the road. You should give yourself at least an hour to an hour and a half for the drive to the trailhead described below.

GETTING THERE

To get to the Brewer Creek Trailhead (7,200 feet) from the town of McCloud, drive east on Highway 89 for 2.8 miles to Pilgrim Creek Road (Road 13), you will see a sign that says Mt. Shasta Wilderness; turn to your left and follow that road for 7.1 miles (past the Clear Creek turnoff) to Sugar Pine Butte Road (Road 19) and turn left. From this point to the trailhead, the route is marked with roadside direction signs. It is approximately 12 more miles to the trailhead. You can also take an optional route by taking Highway 97 from the city of Weed to the Military Pass Road and continue past the turnoff to the Northgate Trailhead. This way is more complex and we recommend that you refer to a Shasta

Trinity National Forest Service road map. The following routes can be reached from this Trailhead: Hotlum-Wintun Ridge, Wintun Glacier, and Hotlum Glacier.

HITTING THE TRAIL

The Brewer Creek trail begins at the signs to the right of the bathroom. This is a very nice trail that meanders through some pine forest while gaining elevation rather slowly and trends to the southwest. After several switchbacks the trail takes a steady southerly direction

Hiking cross country to the Base Camp for the Hotlum Wintun Route

through a bunch of White Bark pines while the views of Mt. Shasta begin to open up. After having crossed several dried up ravines you will come to Brewer Creek itself which, depending on the time of year, should have water flowing in it. At this point you will turn to the right and head directly up the Brewer Creek drainage towards the mountain. Once you reach 9,000 feet, camping sites become available. Some of the better tent sites are found above the first major snowfield at approximately 10,000 feet.

THE CLIMB

The route leaves off from here and continues up following

the broad snowfields between the Hotlum and Wintun
Glaciers. Once you reach 12,400 feet on the main snowfield
you come up against the actual Hotlum/Wintun ridge. At
this point the more popular direction to go is to traverse to
the south towards the upper snowfields that are to the right
of the Wintun Glacier. Turn up towards the right and pass a
solitary rock outcropping to the left called Ship Rock.
Continue heading up keeping the main ridge on your right
until you encounter the Summit snowfield just below the
Summit. Head up to the right and gain the ridge, then head
left and ascend up to the Summit pinnacle. The descent is
the same as the ascent.

SKIING DESCENTS

Affectionately known as the East Face, the descent for the
Hotlum - Wintun starts directly from the Summit block and
descends for over 7,000 feet. When snow levels go all the
way to the parking lot this is one of the longest skiable lines
in the United States. Descend to the east just below the
Summit using the rock ridge as a left handrail. The
consistent slope angle and early corn snow make this an
incredibly enjoyable early day descent. Make sure to have
solid navigational skills and use available landmarks as the
parking lot can easily be missed.

SECTION ELEVATION GAIN TIME

Brewer Creek Trailhead to Base Camp	7,300 ft to 10,000 ft	2,700 ft	3-5 hours
Base Camp to Southern Traverse	10,000 ft to 12,400 ft	2,400 ft	3-5 hours
Traverse to Ship Rock	12,400 ft to 13,100 ft	700 ft	2-3 hours
Ship Rock to Summit	13,100 ft to 14,179 ft	1,079 ft	2-3 hours

MT. SHASTA RECREATION & CAMPING

Mt. Shasta and the surrounding area is located in the Shasta-Trinity National Forest. Situated within this magnificent area is a paradise of trees, streams, and high mountain lakes. Most of the mountain lakes can be reached by car or four-wheel drive. There are several maintained campgrounds available for public use within the National Forest boundaries. Campground and recreation information can be obtained from the Ranger Stations located in the cities of Mount Shasta or McCloud. The Ranger Stations carry a selection of maps and books for sale along with several free brochures pertaining to the Wilderness Area and the land within the Shasta-Trinity National Forest in and around Mt. Shasta. Their map show most of the dirt and paved roads leading to the lakes, trailheads and other sites. Information concerning climbing, backpacking, and skiing conditions is available upon request. All phone numbers, websites, and addresses for the following campgrounds and recreation areas are in Appendix A.

CAMPGROUNDS ON THE MOUNTAIN

MCBRIDE SPRINGS - 4,780 feet

The Forest Service maintains two campgrounds located off the Everitt Memorial Highway. The first camp is McBride Springs located at the 5-mile marker about 5 plus miles from the Bunny Flat trailhead. There are restrooms and drinking water available, and nine sites available. The campground is

closed during the winter. Contact the Mt. Shasta Ranger
Station in regards to availability and the overnight fee.

PANTHER MEADOWS -7,500 feet

The second and most spectacular campground is Panther
Meadows located close to mile 13, about two miles above
Bunny Flat. This camp has a parking lot with a short walk to
the 10 walk-in campsites. There are maintained pit toilets,
fire-rings and tables. Bring your own water to purify the
creek water. The stay limit is three days with no overnight
fee required with first come first served. The view is splendid
and the camp is protected from the wind; although the
nights do get cold here, even during the summer. Because of
the fragile nature of the meadows, great care must be given
by all who visit not to incur damage. In recent years a major
effort has been made by local tribes, volunteers, and the
Forest Service to re-vegetate the native species and improve
the trail system. This camp is only accessible by skis or
snowmobiles during the winter, and on heavy snow years,
the road leading to the camp may not be open till
midsummer.

SAND FLAT - 6,800 feet

Another site available for
camping is at the Sand Flat
trailhead located about a
mile below Bunny Flat.
There are two parking lots,
each a mile apart, and both
have a dirt road which form
a loop leading to Sand Flat.
During the summer, the Flat

makes for an excellent overnight camp and the trail leading out of the flat merges with the Bunny Flat trail to Horse Camp. If you plan on camping there, check with the Ranger Station to see if the snow has melted from the area. This is the best campsite for acclimatization prior to climbing Mt. Shasta. Note: There is no water, tables, or fire-rings; it's basic guerilla camping

BUNNY FLAT - 6,860 feet

Some climbers arriving to the Bunny Flat Trailhead late in the day sometimes just pitch a tent in the Bunny Flat parking lot. This will suffice for an overnight stay if you're in a pinch, although it is not encouraged for more than a quick night's sleep. Camping is allowed inside the National Forest which means you can pitch a tent almost anywhere around the Bunny Flat area. Camping is also allowed inside the Wilderness Area as long as you have your permit with you. Check with the Ranger Station to see if campfire permits are required.

POPULAR RECREATIONAL SITES IN THE MT. SHASTA AREA

LAKE SISKIYOU - 3,200 feet

If you would like to spoil yourself with all the comforts of home, then you may want to consider staying at the fully facilitated Lake Siskiyou Camp Resort. This pristine mountain lake and adjacent Camp Resort is enjoyed by local residents, the Interstate-5 traveler, and destination tourists from near and far. The resort is located on the south shore of Lake Siskiyou on a county road. To get there from Mount Shasta City, take Lake St. west across I-5 to Old Stage Rd., turn left, staying right at the fork of the road. You will now be on W. A. Barr Rd.; continue driving south over Box Canyon Dam for an additional 1.5 miles until you reach the entrance.

Fed by several, pure mountain streams, the 430-acre recreational and sailing lake, with 10 mph speed limit, offers some of the best bass and trout fishing in northern California. A marina with a bait and tackle shop provides a free boat-launch ramp, handicap fishing dock, and fish cleaning station. Mooring slips, powered patio and fishing boats, and electric bass boats are available for rent.

The swimming and sunbathing beach provides family fun galore. Rental kayaks, canoes, pedal boats, sea cycles, and float toys provide affordable means to cruise the lake at your leisure. Play horseshoes or volleyball or munch at the beach snack bar. Picnic areas near the beach have pay showers available. You can visit their gift shop or grab a deli-sandwich at the grocery store.

The 250-acre pine-covered campground and RV Park provides 360 overnight sites or independent lodging in rental RVs. Staying here will give you a good place to relax after your climb and you can finish your vacation in style. www.lakesis.com or call 530.926.2618 / 888.926.2618

CASTLE LAKE - 5,400 feet

Castle Lake is the largest, deepest, and most captivating alpine lake in the Mt. Shasta area. It is located 11 miles west from the city of Mount Shasta via county paved Castle Lake Road. A Forest Service campground is located just below the lake. The 10-site camp is situated in a wooded area for tent or car campers. There are pit toilets, but no drinking water, therefore camping is free. Water in the creek nearby must be treated. The lake offers fishing, swimming, picnicking and hiking. There is no room for motor homes or trailers, and no motor boats are allowed on the lake.

CASTLE CRAGS STATE PARK - 2,100 feet

Castle Crags is one of California's most scenic state parks with its soaring spires of ancient granite and two miles of the cool, quick-running upper Sacramento River. The park is located about 12 miles south of Mount Shasta on Interstate 5. There are 64 family campsites, each with a table, stove, and a food storage locker. Many of the campsites are large enough to accommodate camp trailers up to 21 feet or motor homes to 24 feet, although no hookups are available and there is no dump station. Combination buildings with restrooms, hot showers, and washtubs are nearby.

There are a number of trails to hike, some gentle and others strenuous. There is a Wilderness Area located outside the park for which you need a permit. This area offers some of the best backpacking around with seven miles of the Pacific Crest Trail running through the park. Castle Dome, part of the Crags, is a rounded granite spire that rises to an elevation of 4,966 feet and resembles Half Dome in Yosemite Valley. After you summit Mt. Shasta you may want to drive to the park and do some rock climbing. You have the option of doing some free climbing or attempting to climb 1,000 feet up the vertical Cosmic Wall.

STEWART MINERAL SPRINGS - 3,900 feet
www.stewartmineralsprings.com

If you really want to treat yourself to a thoroughly relaxing day, then take a trip to Stewart Mineral Springs. It is located about three miles north of the town of Weed on Interstate 5, and then four miles west on Stewart Springs Road. Stewart Mineral Springs is a therapeutic mountain retreat with mineral water that is considered one of the most powerful healing waters in the world. The mineral baths work on the principle of drawing toxins from the body while restoring the body's natural mineral balance.

The bathhouse is surrounded by wide, wooden decks overlooking Parks Creek, where you may sunbathe and relax to the sounds of the rushing stream. In the bathhouse you'll get to sweat in their wood heated sauna, and if you want to further your healing, try out a Native American purification sweat in their sweat lodge. Massage services are available along with occasional workshops and seminars. They also offer lodgings which range from sleeping in an authentic Native-American tepee to a luxurious A-frame house. They have the facilities to handle large groups and depending upon the size of the group, they may open the vegetarian restaurant.

DAY-HIKES ON THE MOUNTAIN

Mt. Shasta does not have many marked trails, but some of the more popular day-hikes start from the trailheads. From the Bunny Flat trailhead at 6,860 feet, you can hike in any direction you choose. The most popular hike is the trail to Horse Camp. From Horse Camp you can plan your own route either to Hidden Valley at 9,200 feet, or Helen Lake at

10,443 feet, or maybe just a good hike to one of the ridge tops. Another popular hike is on the Everitt Memorial Highway past the locked gate to the luscious upper Panther Meadow at 7,770 feet. From the Meadow you can take the trail leading up to Grey Butte at 8,108 feet, or continue along the road to the old Ski Bowl at 7,800 feet. From the Ski Bowl you have the option of hiking to the alpine Squaw Valley Meadows at 8,000 feet, or to the little summit of Green Butte at 9,193 feet. Check with the Ranger Station to see if the gate is open.

SOUTHWEST SIDE / BUNNY FLAT

The wildflowers in Panther Meadows used to flourish until heavy recreational traffic destroyed them over the years. The upper part of Panther Meadows has a particular hardy spring that keeps the ground saturated allowing some of the wildflowers to regain their dominance once again. There are marked trails that lead through the meadows and visitors must not wander off them. These meadows are considered spiritual places and most people go there to meditate or to just sit and relax. The trail to Squaw Valley Meadows can be reached from the Gray Butte trail at lower Panther Meadow or from the old Ski Bowl parking lot. Starting from the old Ski Bowl you will see a rock-lined trail leading up the right side of the bowl. One of Shasta's most hardy wildflowers, the western anemone, with its six white petals, locally called the Windflower, grows abundantly in the rocks and sand. Follow this trail over the barren rocky landscape for approximately 1.5 miles until you see a massive rocky butte known as Red Butte at 8,377 feet. You may lose the trail for a short distance through the sandy flat below Red Butte until you pick it up again at The Gate (refer to a topographical map). The Gate is so named because it is a natural passage way between Sargents Ridge and Red Butte. Once you pass through The Gate and drop down the canyon below Sargents Ridge, the landscape gives way to a thick forest of mountain hemlocks and some Shasta Red firs. Follow the well-marked trail for less than a mile until you hear the sound of some rushing streams at which time you will arrive at the upper Meadow.

Looking above the green luscious Meadow at the mountain, you will have a fantastic view of Konwakiton Glacier. The upper Meadow and the surrounding ridges are decorated with a variety of Shasta's wildflowers. The very rare wildflower, Wilkins' harebell, with its five petals and violet-colored cups, grows mostly next to the creeks and in the rocky crevices along the edge of the Meadow. This particular flower only grows for a couple of months during the frost-free season and it's so delicate that one step along the side of it will kill it forever. The upper Meadow and its waters are sometimes disturbed by groups making bathing pools in the creeks. When this happens it backs up the upper natural flow of water and significantly alters the growth of the wildflowers. The meadows are truly a beautiful place on the mountain and we all need to treat them as such.

Before you leave the upper Meadow, you may want to take a short side trip to lower Squaw Valley Meadow. There is usually a well-worn foot trail leading south down the canyon from the upper Meadow which follows along the fast moving Squaw Valley Creek. The lower Meadow with its waterlogged ground is situated in a small basin that usually holds pockets of snow up until midsummer. This area is protected from the wind, and on a hot day the humidity seems to rise which makes the Meadow a perfect place for mosquitos to breed.

THE NORTHEAST SIDE

The Brewer Creek Trailhead at 7,200 feet can provide you access to the Hotlum and Wintun Glaciers. The Northgate Trailhead at 6,900 feet offers the best access to the Whitney, and Chicago Glaciers. Brewer Creek was named in the late 1800's, after William H. Brewer, who was in charge of the Northern California portion of the California State Geologic Survey. The roads leading into the trailheads can be confusing, watch for the marked turn-off . Having a Shasta-Trinity National Forest map is always helpful. Once you arrive at the trailhead, you will find a fairly well marked trail that will lead you to timberline; you should have basic navigation skills to reach the glacier via cross-country routes that vary from year to year. All of these spectacular glaciers can be reached in several hours, however, these hikes are very strenuous and trekking on the glaciers should only be done using rope travel by experienced climbers.

THE SOUTHEAST SIDE

The Clear Creek trailhead 6,480 feet, is located on the southeast side of the mountain. This trail offers solitude for the hiker or climber and it's similar to the trail to Horse Camp because it takes you through some of the mountain's pristine timber country. This trail passes above Mud Creek Falls located in the most scenic and spectacular canyon on the mountain. Mud Creek canyon in some places is more than 1,000 feet deep, extending up to the top of the Red Banks. Once you're at timberline, you have the option of climbing the rugged rocky Wintun Ridge to Wintun Glacier or you can traverse along Clear Creek's gentle slopes to the head of Mud Creek Glacier. Konwakiton Glacier is in full view from the Clear Creek route. Watkins Glacier is within a day's reach for anyone looking for a strenuous climb.

OFF THE MOUNTAIN

It's very rewarding to spend time hiking on Mt. Shasta, but it also can be gratifying when you're hiking on one of the surrounding mountains and look back at the panoramic view of Mt. Shasta. There are numerous hiking trails for those of all ages. For the hardcore backpacker, your opportunity for exploration is endless.

The mountainous area around Mt. Shasta has some alpine lakes that are accessible only on foot. Most of these lakes have trails running to them and some are accessible from the Pacific Crest Trail (PCT). The PCT is one of just a few National Scenic Trails. It runs from Mexico north through the Sierras, winding through the Mt. Shasta area (just south through the Castle Crags area) and north into Oregon, Washington, and finally terminating on the Canadian border. There are several guidebooks covering northern California's trails found in and around the Mt. Shasta area.

AFTERWORD

Congratulations on reading this book! It is our sincere hope that this book has been of value to you whether you are a budding novice climber or a seasoned veteran of the mountains. Always remember that mountaineering is a journey and this book is just one of many sources of information and knowledge that you will need to gather to safely make that journey.

As you begin your journey to climb Mt. Shasta you will most likely meet other like-minded individuals along the way who share the same goals as yourself. You will find that rock climbers, mountaineers, and backcountry skiers are of a very special breed. They all have a healthy respect for the mountain as well as for each other, because one never knows when you may have to help or rely on other climbers to help you.

As you are ascending the mountain, ask yourself: What is the compelling force that is driving you to the Summit? There may be several reasons, or maybe just one, but whatever the reason, remember that it is the journey that counts, not the end result. Enjoy the experience and never forget about the safety of yourself and others. We hope to see you on the mountain someday, or even better yet, up on the Summit.

APPENDIX A

RESOURCES & INFORMATION

Visitors Information: the towns of McCloud, Weed, Dunsmuir, and Mount Shasta City surround Mt. Shasta and offer a wealth of resources for climbers and skiers. The area offers many motels, cabins, bed & breakfast inns, lodges, and special retreats for those who want a comfortable night's sleep before climbing the Mountain or you may look a little further and find a vacation home.

If you like clean air, mountain forest, and no traffic then you may want to consider staying a few nights in one of the campgrounds or state parks nearby. After your climb you may be hungry enough to eat at one of the restaurants located throughout the Mount Shasta area and each town has several different types of restaurants and exquisite cuisines to choose from. Now you may be wondering where you can find all these fine establishments. See the website and resources listed below:

Shasta Chamber of Commerce
www.mtshastachamber.com

South Siskiyou County (Mt. Shasta Area)
www.visitsiskiyou.org

SWS Mountain Guides
www.swsmountainguides.com

RANGER STATIONS:

Mount Shasta Ranger Station
204 West Alma St.
Mount Shasta, CA 96067
(530) 926-4511
Avalanche / Climbing Hotline: (530) 926-9613
www.shastaavalanche.org

McCloud Ranger Station
P.O. Box 1620.
McCloud, CA 96057
(530) 964-2184.

RECREATION:

Mt. Shasta Ski Park
Ski Resort Line: (530) 926-8610
Snow phone: (530) 926-8686
(800) Ski-Shasta (800) 754-7427
www.skipark.com.

Lake Siskiyou Resort
4239 W. A Barr Rd
Mt. Shasta, CA 96067
(530) 926-2618

Stewart Mineral Springs
4617 Stewart Springs Road
Weed, CA 96094.
(530) 938-2222 (800)322-9223
www.stewartmineralsprings.com

Castle Crags State Park
P.O. Box 80.Castella, CA 96017.
(530)235-2684 Reservation Line: (800) 444-7275
www.park.ca.gov

LOCAL MT. SHASTA OUTDOOR RETAILERS:

The Fifth Season
300 N. Mt. Shasta Blvd.
Mount Shasta, CA. 96067.
(530) 926-3606
www.thefifthseason.com.

Shasta Base Camp
308 South Mount Shasta Blvd
Mount Shasta, CA. 96067
(530) 926-2359 / (800) 652-2856
www.shastabasecamp.com

Hermits Hut
3184 Bechelli Lane
Redding, CA 96002.
(800) 507-4455
www.hermitshut.com

WEATHER, AVALANCHE, AND ROAD CONDITIONS:

National Weather Service
24 hour recorded message: (530) 221-5613

Caltrans California Road Conditions:
24 hour recorded message: (800) 427-7623

Local Siskiyou County Road
24 hour recorded message: (530) 842-4438

Website with links to: Weather Avalanche &, Climbing Conditions: www.shastaavalanche.org

APPENDIX B

SWS Mountain Guides & the Authors endorse the following quality mountain equipment companies:

Black Diamond Equipment Inc.
Top of the line Packs, Tents, Skis, & Technical Gear
2084 East 3900 South
Salt Lake City, UT 84124
(801) 278-5533
www.blackdiamondequipment.com

Millet –LaFuma Group
Quality Outdoor Clothing and Equipment
140 Old Laramie Trail Suite 3
Lafayette, CO. 80026
(303) 527-1464
www.millet.fr

Clif Bar & Company
Great selection of Energy Bars for Climbing
1451 66th St.
Emeryville, CA. 94608-1004
www.clifbar.com

Recharge
Great Tasting Natural Sport Drinks
RW Knudsen / Recharge Sports Drinks
1 Strawberry Lane
Orrville, Ohio 44667
www.rwknudsenfamily.com

Point 6 Socks
A great source for quality socks
(877) 949-9665
email:info@point6.com
www.point6.com

Adventure Medical Kits
First rate medical kits for climbers
7700 Edgewater Drive, Suite 526
Oakland, CA. 94624
(510) 261-7414
www.adventuremedicalkits.com

MSR (Mountain Safety Research)
Durable & Efficient Stoves, Water Filters, Sleeping Pads & More
4000 1st Avenue South
Seattle, WA 98134
(206)505-9500
www.cascadedesigns.com

While not endorsed by **SWS Mountain Guides** or the **Authors** the following websites are recommended as a place to purchase quality outdoor equipment.

www.sierratradingpost.com
Good deals on all types of Mountaineering Equipment and Clothing

www.backcountry.com
Good deals on all types of Mountaineering Equipment and Clothing

www.brooks-range.com
Great selection of Mountaineering Equipment and Specialty items

APPENDIX C

2 DAY or 3 DAY
MT. SHASTA SUMMIT CLIMB EQUIPMENT LIST
AVALANCHE GULCH
Courtesy of SWS Mountain Guides
Printable copy is available online at
www.swsmtns.com/mtshastaSummit.html

It is extremely important to the success and safety of your climb that you BRING ALL THE ITEMS LISTED BELOW. Due to the strenuous nature of these climbs, it is MOST IMPORTANT that you pack WELL and pack LIGHT. The weather on Mt. Shasta can be either very warm or very windy and cold - it is usually both! Be prepared to encounter all types of conditions.

PLEASE NOTE: There are lots of **substitutions** available on this equipment list. We use this list from **May through September.** You are **not** **required** to purchase the exact items, BUT YOU DO NEED to bring quality substitutions. We do require **4 layers on top** and **2-3 layers on the bottom plus hats, gloves, sunglasses and the other items on the list!** If you cannot decide on an item or items, feel free to throw it in the car and have the guide help you with the decision at the pack check. If you have any questions about what to bring, **PLEASE,** give us a call at 888-797-6867.

EQUIPMENT

Mountaineering Boots - Modern leather hybrid (**Scarpa™ Summit GTX**) or Plastic Double Boots (**Scarpa™ Inverno, Omega**)

- ❑ Sleeping Bag (Rated to 10-20 degrees, synthetic or down)
- ❑ Full length Sleeping Pad
- ❑ Internal Frame Pack 4,500 - 6,000 cubic inch volume
- ❑ Tent - 3-4 season tent recommended (**Black Diamond™ Bomb Shelter)**
- ❑ Stove (MSR Whisper Lite)
- ❑ Fuel (5-6 oz per person per day)
- ❑ Cooking pot large enough to melt snow
- ❑ Lighter to start the stove

OUTER SHELL LAYER

- ❏ Parka - Gore-Tex™ or equivalent (**Millet™ Point Break Jacket**)

Note: With attached hood that is large enough to fit over all insulating layer(s) and helmet

- ❏ Pants or Bibs Gore-Tex or equivalent
  Note: Side zippers are a highly recommended feature for ventilation and for taking them on or off over heavy boots and crampons.
- ❏ Gore-Tex© Gloves or Mitts with windproof shells or equivalent (**Black Diamond™ Guide Gloves**)
- ❏ Calf Height or Full Length Gaiters (**Black Diamond™ GTX Front Point Gaiters**)

UNDERWEAR

- ❏ Synthetic base layer or wool long john Top – Light weight or mid weight
- ❏ Synthetic base layer or wool long john Bottoms – Light weight to mid weight

INSULATING LAYERS

- ❏ Fleece or Down Jacket (**Millet™ Alpine Down**)
- ❏ Extra Synthetic Top (expedition weight recommended) or Fleece sweater, or wool shirt, or equivalent
- ❏ Medium weight synthetic running tights or light fleece pants or synthetic pants
- ❏ Bibs or Full zip Gore Tex™ pants: **recommended for early season (May or early June) or late season (Late September or October) climbing**
- ❏ 2-3 pairs Wool or Thermal Heavyweight Socks - No Cotton (**Point6 ™Trekking Tech Heavy**)
- ❏ 2-3 pairs Wool or Light Liner Socks – No Cotton!!! (**Point6 Trekking Tech Heavy**)
- ❏ Wool or Synthetic Gloves light liner type (**Black Diamond™ liner gloves**)
- ❏ Wool or Pile Hat - Note: a lightweight balaclava is a great idea for sleeping comfort

OTHER IMPORTANT STUFF:

- ❏ Nylon stuff sacks for gear organization (enough for all equipment)
- ❏ 3 - one liter, wide-mouth, water containers (no runner's or bike bottles please!) *A hydration system such as Camelback may substitute for all but one wide mouth container.
- ❏ Swiss Army-Type Knife or small pocket knife
- ❏ Good quality (DARK) mountaineering sunglasses with side shields
- ❏ Insulated cup and spoon

- ❑ Small plastic bowl (lightweight)
- ❑ Sun block (Rated 25+)
- ❑ Chapstick
- ❑ Long-sleeved light colored t-shirt and bandana (for the hot approach)
- ❑ Shorts (for the hot approach)
- ❑ Sunhat
- ❑ Headlamp (**Black Diamond™ Icon**)
- ❑ Toothbrush and toothpaste
- ❑ Small First Aid Kit with personal medicines
- ❑ Foam ear plugs-- helps provide a good night's sleep by minimizing tent & tent mate noise
- ❑ Toilet paper
- ❑ Bic lighter
- ❑ "Sports Drink" water additive such as **Recharge™ Powdered Mix**, etc.

CLIMBING EQUIPMENT

- ❑ Ice Ax (with the knowledge on how to use it)
- ❑ Crampons - 12 point hinged or semi-rigid crampons (**Black Diamond™ Sabertooth or Contact crampons**)
- ❑ Helmet (UIAA approved Mountaineering helmet – **Black Diamond™ Half Dome**)
- ❑ Ski poles/ Trekking poles

OPTIONAL

- ❑ Camera/Extra Batteries
- ❑ Map of area (Mt. Shasta Topo)
- ❑ Ski Goggles
- ❑ Balaclava (face mask, nice if it's stormy)
- ❑ Down or Fleece vest: This is nice to have, if your budget allows, but not necessary if you have adequate fleece gear
- ❑ Fleece or Synthetic Pants or Bibs recommended for early season (May or early June) or Late Season (Late September or October)

FOOD
DINNER, BREAKFAST, LUNCHES & SNACKS FOR 2-3 DAYS

Dinners: Rice, Noodles, Soups

Breakfast: Instant Oatmeal, Granola Bars, PopTart™

Hot Drinks: Tea, Coffee, Hot Coco

Lunches and High Carbohydrate Snacks:-Clif Bars ™, Power Bars™, GORP (good old peanuts and raisins), bagels, cheese, salami or jerky, crackers, cookies, candy bars, dried fruit, hard candy, chocolate, and granola bars.

APPENDIX D

WEEKEND FIRST AID KIT

Courtesy of Adventure Medical Kits:

www.adventuremedicalkits.com

Bandage Materials

5   Bandage, Adhesive, Fabric, 1" x 3"

5   Bandage, Adhesive, Fabric, Knuckle

2   Bandage, Conforming Gauze, 3"

2   Dressing, Gauze, Sterile, 2" x 2", Pkg./2

2   Dressing, Gauze, Sterile, 4" x 4", Pkg./2

2   Dressing, Non-Adherent, Sterile, 3" x 4"

Bleeding

1   Gloves, Nitrile (Pair), Hand Wipe

1   Instructions, Easy Care Bleeding

1   Trauma Pad, 5" x 9"

Blister / Burn

1   Glacier Gel (Large Oval)

11   Moleskin, Pre-Cut & Shaped (11 pieces)

CPR

1   CPR Face Shield, Laerdal

Duct Tape

1   Duct Tape, 2" x 5 Yards

Fracture / Sprain

1   Bandage, Elastic with Velcro, 3"

1   Bandage, Triangular

1   Instructions, Easy Care Fracture & Sprain

Instrument

1   EMT Shears, 4"

1   Pencil

3   Safety Pins

1   Splinter Picker/Tick Remover Forceps

3   Thermometer, Disposable

Medical Information

1   Comp. Guide to Wilderness & Travel Medicine

1   Patient Assessment Form

Medication

2   Acetaminophen (500 mg), Pkg.

2   Antihistamine (Diphenhydramine 25 mg)

1   Aspirin (325 mg), Pkg./2

2   Ibuprofen (200 mg), Pkg./2

Wound Care

6   After Cuts & Scrapes Antiseptic Wipe

1   Cotton Tip Applicator, Pkg./2

1   Instructions, Easy Care Wound

1   Providone Iodine, 3/4 oz

1   Syringe, Irrigation, 20 cc, 18 Gauge Tip

1   Tape, 1" x 10 Yards

2   Tincture of Benzoin Topical Adhesive

1   Wound Closure Strips, 1/4" x 4", Pkg./10

REFERENCES

Bronaugh, E. J. (1915, December) Mazama, Volume IV No. 4, (pp. 20, 21).Portland, Oregon.

Cooke, W. B. (May 1940). Flora on Mt. Shasta (Reprinted from the American Midland Naturalist, Vol. 23, No. 3, pp. 497-572). South Bend, IN: The University Press Notre Dame.

Grayson, Don ed. (1992). Mountaineering: the freedom of the hills (5th ed).Seattle, Washington: The Mountaineers.

Hackett, Peter M.D. (1993). Mountain sickness: prevention, recognition and treatment. Golden, Colorado: American Alpine Club.

Hoblitt, R.P., Miller, C.D. & Scott, W.E. United States Geological Survey Volcanic Hazards with Regard to Sitting Nuclear-Power Plants in the Pacific Northwest (USGS Open-File report 87-297). Vancouver, Washington: USGS Cascade Volcano Observatory

Udvardy, M.D.F. (1977). The Audubon Society Field Guide to North American Birds: Western Region New York: Alfred A. Knopf.

Little, E. L. (1980). The Audubon Society Field Guide to North American Trees: Western Region. New York: Alfred A. Knopf, Inc.

Miller, Dan C. (1980) Potential hazards from future eruptions in the vicinity of Mount Shasta volcano northern California (Geological Survey Bulletin.1503). Washington: US Govt. Printing Office.

Muir, John (1877, September). Harper's New Monthly Magazine, Vol. 55,.No. 328, (pp.521-530).

Niehaus, Theodore F., Ripper Charles L., (1976). Peterson Field Guide Pacific States Wildflowers. Houghton Mifflin Company, Boston, MA.
Stuhl, Edward and Ford, Marilyn C., ed. (1981). Wildflowers of Mount Shasta (pp. 121,71, 118-129) Klamath Falls, Oregon: Clementine Publishing Co.

United States Geological Survey Open-File Report 94-585 US Department of Interior US Geological Survey Cascades Vol. OBS.

Walton, Bruce (1985). MOUNT SHASTA home of the ancients (pp.77-78) Mokelumne Hill, CA: Health Research

Zanger, Michael (1992). Mount Shasta: History, Legend & Lore (pp.31,32,48,50,71,72) Berkeley, California: Celestial Arts Publishing.

Zanger, Michael & Selters, Andy (1989). The Mt. Shasta Book (pp. 42-76).Berkeley, California: Wilderness Press

SUGGESTED READING

There are numerous books available on climbing and mountaineering. The Seattle-based company, "The Mountaineers," publishes the most comprehensive and contemporary source available on mountaineering today. The book is called **"Mountaineering: The Freedom of the Hills,"** and is available at most mountaineering stores or online. It is considered the bible for all forms of climbing. This book is worth your investment and it should be purchased by anyone that plans on continuing with the sport of mountaineering.

For general recreation and hiking trails we recommend the **"Mount Shasta Guide to Fun"** by Robin Kohn. The Mount Shasta Guide to Fun is the most detailed fun guide to outdoor recreation activates in Siskiyou County and the Mt. Shasta area. Great for hikes, scenic spots, driving tours, and much more. Get a copy online at: www.mountshastaguide.com

GLOSSARY

ACCLIMATE: To gradually become accustomed to a new climate, or in mountaineering, a higher altitude.

ALTITUDE: Elevation above mean sea level, usually expressed in feet or meters.

ASCENT: The act of climbing to the top of cliff, mountain, or peak.

AVALANCHE: A mass of snow and/or ice moving down a mountain.

BELAY: To secure a climber, usually with the aid of another climber and ropes.

BASE CAMP: The lowest and largest fixed camp on a mountain ascent.

BERGSCHRUND: Where the glacier ice has pulled away from the rock creating a crevasse. Typically the top most crevasse on a glacier.

BIVOUAC: A forced or unplanned camp, somewhere on the mountain. The mountaineering lingo is "Bivy."

BLIZZARD: 1. A storm with dry, driving snow, strong winds, and intense cold. 2. A cold frosty treat served at DQ™.

CAIRN: A rounded or conical pile of stones built to mark a trail or a monument.

CHIMNEY: A narrow passage or fissure between two rock faces or in a rock formation.

CIRQUE: An amphitheatre-like valley head, formed at the head of a valley glacier by erosion.

CLIMBING: Is the activity of using one's hands and feet to ascend a steep object, hill, or mountain.

CONSOLIDATION: The act of making or becoming solid, or compact and firm.

CORNICE: An overhanging edge of snow on the crest of a mountain or ridge, formed by wind blowing snow over the ridge, typically on the leeward sides of mountains.

CRAMPONS: Traction devices for your feet used to improve mobility on snow and ice. Required equipment on Mt. Shasta.

CREVASSE: A deep crack in an ice sheet or glacier.

CREVICE: A fissure or crack, which forms in rock.

CUMULUS CLOUDS: Large, white, puffy clouds that form rapidly on Mt. Shasta and are an indication of possible thunderstorm and lighting activity. Due to the extreme summer temperature gradients between Mt. Shasta and the heat in the Sacramento Valley. Generally seen in the summer months.

DESCEND: To go down by climbing, rappelling, lowering, or sliding down off a cliff, mountain, or peak.

DESCENT: The act of climbing, rappelling, lowering, or sliding down off a cliff, mountain, or peak.

FAUNA: A collective term for the animals of any given geographical region.

FLANK: The side of a mountain or cliff.

FLORA: The plants native to a certain geographical region or geological period.

FREEZING POINT: Point on a mountain when the air temperature reaches 32 degrees or 0 Celsius. This will vary depending on weather conditions, seasons, and a number of other factors.

FRENCH TECHNIQUE (or flat footing): A crampon technique wherein the spikes of the bottom of the crampons are fully engaged with the snow or ice. Typically used on easier mountain terrain.

FRONT POINTING (or German Technique): A fundamental crampon technique wherein the front two points or spikes are used to ascend moderate to steep snow or ice slopes.

FROSTBITE: The term for damage to skin and other tissues caused by freezing where tissue damage occurs.

FROSTNIP: A mild form of frostbite where no tissue destruction occurs.

FUMAROLES: A small fissure (crack or hole) in a volcano.

FURROW: A deep wrinkle in the bark of a tree.

GAITERS: Garments worn over the boot and lower pant legs. Used primarily to prevent snow and small rocks (scree) from entering the top of the boot.

GERMAN TECHNIQUE (or front pointing): A fundamental crampon technique wherein the front two points or spikes are used to ascend moderate to steep snow or ice slopes.

GLACIER: A large persistent body mass of ice that forms where the accumulation of snow exceeds it melting over many years or centuries. A glacier moves very slowly down a mountain deforming and creating crevasses.

GLISSADE (glissading): Literally to glide, a mountaineering technique for rapid descent on a peak or mountain by sliding down utilizing an ice axe to maintain control and speed of descent.

GULCH: A ravine or deep-walled valley.

GULLY: A small valley or ravine originally worn away by running water and serving as a drainage way after prolonged heavy rain or snow melt.

HYPOTHERMIA: A condition in which the body's core temperature drops below the required temperature for normal metabolism and body functions.

ICE AXE: A multi-purpose ice and snow tool used by mountaineers both in ascent and descent of routes which involve snow and/or ice conditions.

JET STREAM: A narrow band of swiftly moving air found at very high altitudes in the northern hemisphere.

KRUMMHOLTZ: Crooked, bent, or twisted wood (used to refer to Whitebark pines on Mt. Shasta).

LENTICULAR (clouds): Stationary, lens-shaped clouds that form at high altitudes, normally aligned perpendicular to the wind direction. On Mt. Shasta an indication of a "cold and windy Summit."

METEOROLOGIST: A person who gathers and analyzes information on atmospheric conditions. They attempt to spot and interpret trends, understand the weather of yesterday, describe the weather of today, and predict the weather of tomorrow.

MORAINE: Glacial moraines are formed by the deposition of material from a glacier and are exposed after the glacier has retreated. These features appear as linear mounds of non-sorted rock, gravel, and boulders within a matrix of fine powdery material.

MOUNTAINEERING: The sport, hobby, or profession of hiking, skiing, and climbing mountains.

MOUNTAIN RESCUE: Refers to search and rescue activities that occur in a mountainous environment. Mountain rescue services may be paid professionals or trained volunteers.

MUD POTS: A type of hot spring or fumaroles consisting of a pool of usually bubbling mud.

PEAK: "A mountain peak" is a point on the surface that is higher in elevation then all points immediately adjacent to it. Referred to as the Summit.

PINNACLE: A tall pointed formation such as a mountain peak.

PLATEAU: Usually an extensive land area having a relatively level surface raised sharply above the adjacent land.

POSTHOLING: "Lingo" in the sport of mountaineering. It refers to the act of sinking up to your knees, hips, or waist, in soft, melted or powdery snow, i.e. forming a "post hole" after each step.

PRESSURE BREATHING: A method of breathing at altitude by forcing the exhale through pursed lips which causes a slight back pressure allowing for maximizing air intake of oxygen at altitude.

RED BANKS: The name given to the red cliffs that form the head or top of Avalanche Gulch.

REST STEP: A form of resting your leg muscles on steep ground.

RIDGE: A geological feature consisting of a continuous elevated crest for some distance. Ridges are usually termed hill or mountains as well, depending on size.

ROUTE: A specific trail or unmarked path, up a rock or mountain.

SCREE: A pile of debris at the base of a cliff or hill. "Scree" varies in size from pea-size gravel to fist-size cobbles. (See talus)

SELF-ARREST: A mountaineering technique typically using an ice axe in which a climber who has fallen and is sliding down a snow or ice slope arrest or (stops) the slide by him or herself.

SKINS: Used by backcountry skiers "skins" refer to material which is strapped or uses an adhesive to adhere to the bottom of the skis. This enables the skier to climb up a snowfield without slipping.

SLOPE: Or grade of a physical feature, topographical landform refers to the amount of inclination of that surface to the horizontal. Example: Mt. Shasta's average slope angle is 30-35 degrees (angle of repose).

SNOW BANK: A mound or heap of snow or area of snow that the snowplow has pushed up.

SNOW BRIDGE: Is an arc (bridge of snow) across a crevasse, a crack in rock or a creek, or some other opening in terrain. Snow bridges can present a danger as it creates the illusion of unbroken surface while hiding the opening under a layer of snow of unknown thickness.

SNOW FIELD: A permanent accumulation of snow and ice, typically found below the snowline. Glaciers originate in snowfields.

SNOW LINE: The climatic snow line is the point above which snow and ice cover the ground throughout the year. The actual snow line may seasonally be significantly lower or higher.

SUMMIT: The highest point, peak, or "top" of a mountain.

SUN-CUPS: An area of a snowfield or glacier which on clear days the surface snow melts at different rates due to several factors. Sun-cups can grow over 2 feet in height on Mt. Shasta. They can be very difficult to climb through and ski over.

TALUS: "Talus or Scree" is the generic name for broken rock fragments at the base of crags or mountains. The two terms are often interchangeable, though scree commonly refers to smaller material like mixed gravel and loose dirt while talus refer to rock larger then scree. Mt. Shasta has an abundance of both.

TEPHRA: Molten or solid rock particles of all sizes from boulders to dust, which are erupted into the atmosphere from a volcano.

TREE LINE: The edge of the habitat at which trees are capable of growing (usually due to cold temperatures or lack of moisture). Mt. Shasta's timberline is approximately 8,000 feet depending on aspect. Also referred to as "Timberline."

TOPOGRAPHIC MAP: A type of map characterized by large-scale detail and quantitative representation of relief, usually using contour line in modern mapping. Typical map preferred by mountain hikers and mountaineers.

TRAILHEAD: The beginning or start of a trail.

TRAVERSE: To hike or climb at an angle across a slope. Example: we have to "traverse" (cross) this slope.

VESTIBULE: A floorless covered section located outside a tent entrance that is typically used for storage of boots, packs, and other equipment not needed inside the tent.

VOLCANO: An opening in the crust of the earth from which heated solid, liquid, or gaseous matters are ejected.

VOLCANO VENT: An area or opening on a volcano that allows heat, liquid, and gas to escape.

WANDS: Typically, 2-3 foot long bamboo dowels or rods with brightly colored surveyor tape attached to the top and are placed in the snow to mark the route and hazards up a mountain.

WHITE-OUT: A weather condition in which visibility and contrast are severely reduced by clouds and/or snow.

INDEX

ABOUT THE AUTHORS

David Cressman is a Co-Owner of SWS Mountain Guides, having over 150 Summits on Mt. Shasta and 70 on Mt. Whitney and has extensive high altitude experience and has lead countless international expeditions in Ecuador, Bolivia, Russia and Argentina. Dave is a graduate of the 10-day AMGA guide courses in alpine climbing, AMGA Top Rope Site Manager, holds a Wilderness First Responder (WFR), and he is a graduate of the National Avalanche School as well as Avalanche Level I & Level II. During the winter months Dave is a professional ski patroller at the Mt. Shasta Ski Park as well as a PSIA Level I ski instructor/race coach. He graduated from Humboldt University with B.S. Degrees in Biology, Zoology, and Oceanography. Dave lives in Mt. Shasta with his wife Alana. They have three children: Jarrod, Mariah, and Jesse, and his dog Bailey.

Timothy Keating is the founder and Co-Owner of SWS Mountain Guides. He has over 100+ Summits on Mt. Shasta and over 100+ on Mt. Whitney. As an avid backcountry skier, he has logged countless ski ascents on Mt. Shasta, guided international treks and expeditions in Mexico, Ecuador, Peru, Bolivia, Argentina, Tanzania, United Federation of Russia and Nepal. Tim is a graduate of a 10-day AMGA Alpine Guides Course, AMGA Certified Top Rope Site Manager, Professional Climbing Guides Institute Certified Top Rope Guide, Wilderness First Responder, Certified Avalanche Instructor & Professional Member of the American Avalanche Association, a Level III Avalanche Training Certification, Graduate from the National Avalanche School, and Leave No Trace Certified Trainer. Tim has a BA in Geography from Humboldt St. University, speaks Spanish and is married to Emily and they have a son, Joshua and two Samoyeds Misha and Rookie.

"JB" Brown is a Co-Owner of SWS Mountain Guides. He has backpacked and climbed in almost every major range in the western United States. He is a ski instructor for Deer Valley and Jackson Hole Mountain Resort. JB has attained Professional Ski Instructors Association (PSIA) Alpine Instructor level II as well as Certified Backcountry Instructor, Avalanche Level I & Level II, and Level III, Leave No Trace Certifications. He is a member of the AMGA and is in the process of pursuing the international IFMGA certification. JB has a BS in Political Science, speaks Spanish and Nepali and lives with his 12 year old black lab Sully.

Made in the USA
Lexington, KY
19 December 2012